FIRE FRONT

First Nations poetry
and power today

First published 2020 by University of Queensland Press
PO Box 6042, St Lucia, Queensland 4067 Australia
Reprinted 2020 (twice), 2021, 2023

University of Queensland Press (UQP) acknowledges the Traditional Owners and
their custodianship of the lands on which UQP operates. We pay our respects to their
Ancestors and their descendants, who continue cultural and spiritual connections to
Country. We recognise their valuable contributions to Australian and global society.

uqp.com.au
reception@uqp.com.au

Cover illustration by Rachael Sarra
Cover design by Design by Committee (Josh Durham)
Typeset in 11.25/14.5 pt Adobe Garamond Pro by Post Pre-press Group, Brisbane
Printed in Australia by McPherson's Printing Group

The University of Queensland Press is
assisted by the Australian Government
through the Australia Council, its arts
funding and advisory body.

This project is supported by the Copyright Agency's Cultural Fund.

COPYRIGHTAGENCY
CULTURAL FUND

A catalogue record for this book is available from the National Library of Australia.

ISBN 978 0 7022 6272 2 (pbk)
ISBN 978 0 7022 6388 0 (epdf)

University of Queensland Press uses papers that are natural, renewable and recyclable
products made from wood grown in well-managed forests and other controlled
sources. The logging and manufacturing processes conform to the environmental
regulations of the country of origin.

FIRE FRONT

First Nations poetry
and power today

edited by
Alison Whittaker

Contents

Introduction by Alison Whittaker   ix

'Ancestor, you are exploding the wheelie bin'
ESSAY: Dear Ancestor by Chelsea Bond   3

Alexis Wright, *Hey Ancestor!*   9
Lisa Bellear, *Beautiful Yuroke Red River Gum*   15
Jeanine Leane, *The Colour of Massacre*   17
Ali Cobby Eckermann, *Unearth*   19
Natalie Harkin, *Domestic*   20
Archie Roach, *Took the Children Away*   23
Briggs (ft. Gurrumul Yunupingu),
    The Children Came Back   26
Alice Eather, *Yúya Karrabúrra (Fire Is Burning)*   29
Deborah Doorlak L. Moody, *Bilya Kep*   33
Ruby Langford Ginibi, *Black Woman*   34
Jack Davis, *A Letter to the Shade of Charles Darwin*   35

'Despite what Dorothea has said about the sun scorched land'
ESSAY: Too Little, Too Much by Evelyn Araluen   39

Samuel Wagan Watson, *The Grounding Sentence*   46
Lionel Fogarty, *Caused Us To Be Collaborator*   49
Lionel Fogarty, *Connoisseur*   53
Luke Patterson, *Darkinjung Burning*   55
Alison Whittaker, *Many Girls White Linen*   57
Oodgeroo Noonuccal, *Municipal Gum*   59
Diwurruwurru (with Phillip Hall), *Millad Mob Da Best!*   60

Lorna Munro, *YILAALU – BU-GADI*
   (*Once Upon a Time in the Bay of Gadi*)   62
Alf Taylor, *Moorditj Yorgah*   65
Kevin Gilbert, *The New True Anthem*   66
Elizabeth Hodgson, *Boots*   68

'I say rage and dreaming'

ESSAY: Bleat Beneath a Blanket by Bruce Pascoe   71

Joel Davison, *Ngayrayagal Didjurigur (Soon Enough)*   76
Ellen van Neerven, *Expert*   78
Evelyn Araluen, *Dropbear Poetics*   80
Charmaine Papertalk Green, *Honey to Lips Bottlebrush*   82
Elizabeth Jarrett, *Invasion Day*   84
Mojo Ruiz de Luzuriaga, *Native Tongue*   86
Steven Oliver, *Why Not Be Brothers and Sisters?*   88
Kerry Reed-Gilbert, *Got Ya*   90
Declan Furber Gillick, *Nanna Emily's Poem*
   (*Mount Isa Cemetery 2014*)   92
Romaine Moreton, *Are You Beautiful Today?*   96
Meleika Gesa-Fatafehi, *Say My Name*   105

'Because we want it back, need it back, because they can'

ESSAY: Lead You to the Shore by Steven Oliver   109

Claire G. Coleman, *I Am the Road*   117
Ken Canning/Burraga Gutya, *Old Clever Woman*   120
Pansy Rose Napaljarri, *The Changing Face*
   of the Jukurrpa   123
Paul Collis, *Cult-charr Jammer*   127

Jim Everett, *Move on Black*   129
Pauline Whyman, *Chocolate Wrappers*   131
Yvette Holt, *Custodial Seeds*   133
Tony Birch, *Visiting*   134
Kevin Buzzacott, *Lake Eyre Is Calling: Ankaku for Life*   135
Provocalz and Ancestress, *Behind Enemy Lines*   136

'This I would tell you'

ESSAY: Medicine In, Obligation Out
   by Ali Cobby Eckermann   143

Oodgeroo Noonuccal, *Son of Mine*   148
Elizabeth Walker, *Grandfather of Mine*   149
Melanie Mununggurr-Williams, *I Run ...*   150
Sachem Parkin-Owens, *My Ancestors*   152
Dylan Voller, *Justice for Youth*   154
Laniyuk, *Remember*   155
Kirli Saunders, *Wirritjiribin*   157
Raelee Lancaster, *Haunted House*   158
Baker Boy (ft. Dallas Woods), *Black Magic*   160
Maggie Walsh, *Better Put the Billy On*   165

Notes on Sources   169
Acknowledgements   177

Introduction
ALISON WHITTAKER

It licks at the edges of the colonisers' language. It hems it into a workable, imperfect shape. It tears through the settlers' plantations, their arrangements of the trees and their form. It takes its restorative heat to the right flora, which release their seeds and bear down hard for the burn. It loosens and enriches nutrients from the top of the ecology. It brings them down to bring other things up. *Fire Front*, a thin and precise incision into the colonial Australian imagination, is ready when the wind changes. When the wind changes, everything that is burning becomes the front. Big. Bigger and more powerful than we could have ever envisioned.

It's a cliché to say that Indigenous poetry is powerful. From where does that power come? Like *Fire Front*, does it come from challenging and subverting the English language, or the poetic forms and traditions of the West? Or does it come from creating space for other ways of thinking and rethinking and returning to proper thought? Does it nurture its Indigenous readers? In this collection, you will find fifty-three poems fuelling, making space for, depriving, reshaping, undermining and doing power in every way. What they have in common is why they do it: for the emancipation of First Nations.

Selecting poems for this collection was a challenge. Poetics are practised extensively by our communities – across oral storytelling, embedding storytelling insights into Language itself, music and song, conversational wordwork, published poetry with major publishing houses, small press poetry, self-published print poetry, slam poetry, protest poetry, performance poetry. How to curate a collection of just fifty-three poems for all of this? I have certainly made mistakes in doing so – first and foremost, in trying to. This anthology is only a sample – taking a hand and grazing it over the tip of a fire to blister it up in the shape of the big sovereign renaissance happening right now.

It is necessarily incomplete. It sits alongside and owes much to such strong anthologies as *Inside Black Australia* (edited by Uncle Kevin Gilbert), *Us Mob Writing* (edited by Aunty Kerry Reed-Gilbert), *Paper Dreaming* (edited by Lorna Munro), *The Macquarie PEN Anthology of Aboriginal Literature* (edited by Anita Heiss and Peter Minter), *All Ginibi's Mob* (edited by Aunty Ruby Langford Ginibi) and more ephemeral ways that we bring our poetry together like *Black Rhymes Poetry Night* (convened by a matriarchal collective and administered by Evelyn Araluen and Lorna Munro), *Woman's Way* (compiled by NITV), and *Poetry in First Languages* (co-ordinated by Kirli Saunders). There are others, whose names may have slipped this page, who have done such significant work that it would be an honour for *Fire Front*, too, to one day slip in a collective memory while the imprint of the works contained therein remain. It should be read as such, as a reference point and not an authority – especially because these poems appeared previously (performed, online, winning prizes, or in print) and can be found elsewhere. Just grazing your hand, reader, over this fire.

The collection, where possible, has fallen into five different kinds of firepower, articulated by muscular and nurturing figures in their respective field of Indigenous poetics.

In 'Ancestor, you are exploding the wheelie bin' – poets work out their relationships to ancestors, kin and Country in the circumstances and violence of colony. In 'Despite what Dorothea has said about the sun scorched land' – poets write about resisting directly settler imposition on Indigenous Country and bodies. In 'I say rage and dreaming' – poets envision ways of speaking back and speaking to one another. In 'Because we want it back, need it back, because they can' – poets account for loss and plan for repair. And, finally, in 'This I would tell you' – new shoots of poetry emerge, directly nurtured by one another.

Fire Front also acknowledges that the fire of poetry is fundamentally relational. There is someone who is spoken to, and someone who is the speaker, sure – but there is also someone who is made responsible to the work and someone who is made responsible by the work, and an ecological sense that all this poetry relates to and enables the other. Fundamentally relational also means fundamentally intergenerational. Some of the poets in here have gone to be with their ancestors. Some have written down to their descendants, and others have written up as descendants.

How *Fire Front* relates is not just to other kin and countrypeople – but to a bigger diplomatic sense of how First Nations relate to one another, how the Fire moves responsibly. *Fire Front* is fundamentally, not as a footnote but in a way that is difficult to convey in this colonial language, about Country and everything contained and woven and moved into it. It can burn nowhere else, and with nothing else, and for nothing else.

The relationality of *Fire Front* is also not only good ways – but fundamentally addresses the question of the coloniser, how to tussle with the settler colony, and to account for just what both have wrought on us. The Fire is as much a threat of reckoning with what is improperly imposed, as it is an offer for restoration. It is insurrectionist.

As is evident in how I must always say 'and also', the Fire is also plural – as internally diverse as the poets themselves. Not just in what the poets bring to the work as holders of its fire, but in the style of their burn, their use of language, their articulated purpose. *Fire Front* contains poems written from inside the colonial front of the prison, written for performance in the streets, performed as rap and song, entered into as a scholarly exercise, launched into prizes like the Nakata Brophy Short Fiction and Poetry Prize for Young Indigenous Writers and the Judith Wright Poetry Prize, and ever more reasons not subject to the gaze of the public record – healing, reeling, revealing.

It is easy to fall into the trap of calling everything Indigenous endlessly excellent, when what is at stake is not just that it is excellent but why, but the works contained herein are the sharp front of blak poetry. They are, to understate things, really good.

What is clear is that Indigenous poetry is a collective task, passing the Fire from one front to another, and so this introduction can't stand alone or claim to speak for any of the poems.

So it won't, except to offer deep gratitude to each poet for weaving together something with English words and Language and all the ephemera and fraughtness of poetry that did the great thing of meaning something to First Nations peoples and societies. It is an honour to host your works here, to maybe offer them to burn within new audiences, and if nothing else, to serve as a collective memory of your wordwork and its burning power.

To pass on their insight, five Indigenous public intellectuals – Associate Professor Chelsea Bond, Professor Bruce Pascoe, Steven Oliver, Evelyn Araluen and Professor Ali Cobby Eckermann – have shared their responses to the works contained.

Bond reminds us of the mandate our ancestors bestow upon us to bear witness, bear warmth and stand firm as the forests churn around us. Pascoe takes us to the foundation of wordwork from our Old People – and muses on how and why we honour and continue that in our storm of desolation, fury, disappointment. Oliver speaks to poetry as if it were a mirror, a generous reader who knows the contours of our listening practices well. Cobby Eckermann takes us to the very question of why we write – to the future, to heal, to publish, to burn – and what it means to linger in the certain uncertainty of poetry. Araluen takes her literature scholar's gaze so lovingly and exactingly to the poets assigned her that it would be a disservice to summarise it here.

Let their words, not mine, shape how you read the poems in *Fire Front*.

Their words reflect what First Nations poets have known for the long, long time behind us and beyond us: that poetry is for any and all purposes and has enduring relevance and resonance in First Nations and our societies. It burns, for all its diversity, with great deliberateness, purpose and precision. It burns for us.

'Ancestor, you are exploding the wheelie bin'

— Alexis Wright, 'Hey Ancestor!'

Dear Ancestor
CHELSEA BOND

~~Homo Erectus.~~	People.
~~Cannibals.~~	Warriors.
~~Baboons.~~	Survivors.
~~A Real Live Golliwog.~~	Old Song Woman.
~~Poor Miserable Halfstarved Bottlenosed Caricatures Of Humanity.~~	Mob.
~~Brute Man.~~	Dad.
~~Gins.~~	Mother.
~~Waitresses.~~	Children.
~~Domestics.~~	Elders.
~~Aborigines.~~	Ancestors.

Dear Ancestor,

Of all the things you have been called, I will write to you in the name you must be known by. Ancestor. And I will write to you via the relationship by which you are known to me and through me.

My father's name was Vern Watego. He passed eleven years ago.
His mother was Amelia Slockee. She passed three years ago.
Her mother was Clara Williams. She passed before I was born.
Her mother was Emily Jackey and she was born in the middle of the century before last.

Her father was Bilin. They said he was the last of his tribe.

They were wrong, as you well know.
Ngulli yahnbai gulli bahn! [We are still here now!]

But what does it mean to be *here*? *now*?

It certainly is a strange predicament to know oneself only as far back as that Ancestor that they insisted, among other things, was the last of us. My body here, now, in its being, tells the truth about our ongoing existence, or at least it tries to, every damn day.

I want to talk truth, not about it, rather I want to talk to you truthfully, Ancestor. To speak truthfully, to externalise that internal dialogue, demands of us a public outing of our vulnerability. It's something that I've typically resisted, not because I prefer lies, but because I want something to be sacred, reserved just for us. But maybe too I'm more familiar with a public truth-telling that relies too heavily upon strength in insisting upon our persistence as a people. I think I almost forgot that vulnerability was not weakness but an expression of our humanity too, in this place, here, now.

I remember when my dad passed away, I didn't just grieve the loss of him, I also mourned the loss of no longer being known as one of Vern's girls. For some reason, I thought that when he died, so too did my belonging, that my ancestry was somehow more faint. But it didn't die or fade, it was my enactment of it that had to change. It meant that when family gathered, I would not follow in behind him, I now would sit at the adults' table where he once sat. When my nanna passed a few years later, I realised that I no longer had living Elders in terms of my immediate family tree. When I grieved the loss of her, I also grieved the loss of answers to questions that I never took the time to ask. I grieved the loss of stories that are now just pieces of which I can no longer go back and check to restore them whole, to be retold in full. Throughout my life my Aboriginal ancestry was known through them, their stories, their experiences and their connections to place. But they are gone.

I am still here, now.

It really is a most daunting prospect, the realisation of being the latest living Ancestor in your family tree. For too many of our families, we find ourselves made Elders before our time, simply because we are the last ones living here, now. To think of oneself in this way is not a hierarchical position within one's family tree. No, it is a reminder of our mortality and eternity. To be the next, in regards to our proximity to that soil, the next to be returned to it, no longer as seed but as the root that sustains that age-old tree forever more. Neither last, or lost, but forever.

The latest living Ancestor, here, now, carries a responsibility not just of living, but to think deeply about what legacy will be left in that living. For it is our living, here, now, that will determine the strength of that tree, whether it will continue to grow, even when the soil isn't particularly fertile, especially because it isn't, here, now.

You see, they want so much for us not to be here, in fact that is what they have always wanted. In being named Aborigines, they sought to remake us as a doomed people, destined to die out, knowing us as anything but human.

How does one thrive in a world that wishes us dead?

I can't help but think of the buttress roots that are in abundance on Mount Tamborine that sustain ancient trees in the thinnest of soils. You see those roots are as smart as they are strong, in seeking out the nutrients the tree needs, they grow taller above the soil, rather than digging deep down into it. Not only do they buttress those age-old trees, but they too grow wide so as to support those weaker trees that don't have the same support.

I think to be a good Ancestor is to be like the buttress root. But if I am honest with you, most days I'm not sure what that looks like here, now. I wish I could live in that future time where I could see whether I was the right kind of Ancestor in the moment I was called to be in this place, if indeed I was everything you asked of me.

Maybe then you could tell me if I let you down when I couldn't see a brand new day. You could tell me if I failed in my failing to see possibilities in this place. Did I not have enough joy? Should I have laughed or danced more? Should I have rested more, learned more, given more? Should I have fought more?

Just as the buttress root cannot go deep beneath the soil, nor can it climb to the canopy to see how high the tree it sustains will reach. I'm left to pretend that I know. I rely on the feeling of the force of those behind me. I too feel the weight of those I am meant to carry. Some days it feels too heavy. Some days it feels too lonely. Some days I'm tired of fighting, of having to search out nourishment in this soil, of pursuing a thing called justice so stubbornly despite not yet knowing what it actually is.

But I remind myself, those feelings of loneliness, hopelessness and uncertainty come from a degraded soil, not a degraded people. A soil that continues to underestimate the wisdom of our roots.

This world will insist that you be a good Aborigine. It will lie to you about who you are, and what is needed to sustain us as a people. But one thing I know here, now, is that no good has ever come from being a good Aborigine. The Aborigine, in its good or bad state, is always dying, lost, and never real enough. But the Aborigine was never real in the first place; it is of their imagining, not ours.

We were made to be good Ancestors.

Good Ancestors sustain the forest that they cannot clear. Good Aborigines, meanwhile, only ever sustain the institutions that insist upon our demise.

And so I tell you this, my dear children, never be the good Aborigines they insist you be, for it is in our being, as Ancestors, here, now, that we are still here, now.

Love from,

Your Mum x

Hey Ancestor!
ALEXIS WRIGHT

Hey ancestor, you talking to me?

Country time everyday.

I know, I know, but wouldn't you know it, it's the 26th of January again, old Whitefella Day.

Party time for some, sad day for others.

Listen! Can't you hear country keeping its peoples' memories beating strongly, everybody heard? It's the pulse of all our broken hearts crying for families lost in the war we keep having, the children we keeps losing.

Those are big memories, far too strong, where spirits cry deep down knowledge of the real title of country. What's to celebrate? Country ripped? Country broken? You looking at all that type of thing? Tens of thousands of years it took for learning that kind of knowledge for managing land right way, waters, the skies, and the stars.

Me! Not bothering too much because I am country.

Country time everyday.

Anyway call it what you like, Australia Day or whatnot?
Mouthing off day. Bugger all day mean nothing to me.
You tell me what's good about nothing? A bit of split second
in the space of time. One day! What for? That's nothing in
the scheme of time that my mob been sitting here, looking
after all this traditionally inter-woven law country, keeping
it strong, every day. You want to beat that first?

That's real sovereignty kind of thinking. True ownership.
Comes with responsibility. Caring. Respect. Stuff like that
for instance.

Permanence – ties unbroken, can't be broken.

Deep roots. Core roots.

Country time everyday.

I am talking about time immemorial experience – how
to grow roots like that. Not like scrap of paper made
yesterday – a second ago, flimsy, impermanence, that type of
thing saying you got the title over blackfella country, you are
on top. That's nothing. You are not owner. Scrap of paper
only painful in the heart, only cover the surface with poison.
It can't get inside proper deep law in my head. Lies type of
thing like that fall apart eventually, eroding unfortunately,
like sickly wind vapouring out of any little whitefella
powerhouse thing called government. That's only tiny. Big
deal. Paper gets blown away. Paper only good for that.

You want to know who's speaking? Me! I got no problem because I am country. I got no paper. Just old man talking about a fact, that's all. Elder of country. A spirit man who manages law stories from time immemorial living in the back of your mind.

Live in a wheelie bin now. Squashed amongst the rubbish, in piles of waste stuff, in ugly thoughts, in mad sweat crawling all over the place like lice. No worry. Any filth like that just dries on my skin, sticks like hot glue in my mind, but I can wait for eternity. Someone will come along and collect the rubbish eventually, and it will be sorted out in one big pile-up down at the tip.

Hey ancestor, while I am talking, I noticed how you have put on a bit of vitriolic weight this year. You look awesome twisting in the sky at sunset. I have been thinking about whether I am dreaming I am you, or are the storm clouds just getting heavier in my mind while sitting around on my spirit country that is being turned into a wheelie bin of rubbish that whitefella say is not mine anymore. What you look like? My spirit brain and yours! How am I going to describe ancestral dreaming inside the old song man spirit, the old song woman, the little kid's static freaking up and down across white nylon billowing over the land – suffocating the life out of country, the kid's target indiscriminate, their mind lost to the incessant barking of dogs.

I watch how you loom wide across the horizon; see how you are thinking as you charge through memory of all my thoughts.

I see that you have come to the celebratory party this year wearing something different, impersonating a super-cell storm body, and in your heart's heat, your aura throwing flames across the landscape. Pretty big look that. Bloody good actor, roaring rapid-fire across the surface of country in such awesomeness, being all visible, all thunder and roaring. Maybe you are searching for a reckoning, maybe payback, maybe retribution, maybe searching for where your story is being hidden, if it is being kept properly, secretly inside the brain of elders – the caretakers, or from where it was stolen from country, if it lies in the graves of family robbed from their potentiality of caring for country, or are you looking for the lies hidden on a piece of paper somewhere, locked in somebody's cupboard.

You seem all radical, in a hurry. The environmental science people said that the freak storms coming more frequently are a consequence of climate change, but I think that your appearance is the result of those little pieces of paper telling lies about land ownership by people who don't know your power. I suppose the ancestral story should look the way you have decided to show yourself, your powerful story of millenniums revealed in full swing.

But you are becoming more enormous and looming right out of control across the land, and controlling my mind. The more you push, the more I can't find the answer for what should be kept under control. Where are all the proper story keepers? Who's going to sing all the sacred story so you won't feel lonely anymore, is there anyone left? Anyone there? Anyone at the birthday party?

Ancestor, you are exploding the wheelie bin. The plastic crap stuff is all over the place and flying with the seagulls in the storm, slapped amongst filthy kimbies, the polystyrene meat trays and empty beer cans, thousands spinning in the atmosphere. The poisonous fumes and acid unleashed. A wild wind is screwing off the tops of trees for kilometres around, and bashing the tree trunks into the ground. Ash clouds preceded a wall of mud water rushing over country, carrying cattle and sheep with trucks and cars past flooded houses. I am only an old man with poor eyesight, but I get the picture. Bloody oath. *Country time everyday.*

You know, and I may be wrong here, but I think you are starting to shake a bit of sense into the heart of what's going on around here, the way you talk about real sovereignty when you show the language of country, the way you broadcast a few fast new stories from the ancestral realm.

There are skinny old hungry foxes having Macca's with the lot for early Australia Day breakfast. And there are ants out there labouring in the dirt under the wings of a dead butterfly, taking it on a journey that seems to take forever, a journey as great as travelling around the world to the butterflies cemetery.

Beautiful Yuroke Red River Gum
LISA BELLEAR

Sometimes the red river gums rustled
in the beginning of colonisation when
Wurundjeri
Bunnerong
Wathauring
and other Kulin nations
sang and danced
and
laughed
aloud

Not too long and there are
fewer red river gums, the
Yarra Yarra tribe's blood becomes
the river's rich red clay

There are maybe two red river gums
a scarred tree which overlooks the
Melbourne Cricket Ground the
survivors of genocide watch
and camp out, live, breathe in various
parks 'round Fitzroy and down
town
cosmopolitan
St Kilda

And some of us mob have graduated
from Koori Kollij, Preston TAFE,
the Melbin Yewni

Red river gums are replaced
by plane trees from England
and still
the survivors
watch.

The Colour of Massacre

JEANINE LEANE

As a new century dawned white Australians were urged
to feel comfortable and relaxed about their history.
'Shake off that irksome black arm band – legacy of radical
lefties who can't leave well enough alone – and their
tiresome chant that white Australia has a Black history and
we all have blood on our hands.
We've got a new song to sing now!'

Right-wing historians hummed the new tune
and set about to write Aboriginal massacres out
of the record, out of the history books, out of the classroom.

There weren't really fifteen thousand Palawa people
in Van Diemen's Land before the arrival of
white Christians. They said.
There weren't even five thousand!
Only a few hundred naked savages roamed here
and a meagre hundred or so killed –
in self-defence – of course.
Or perhaps they were stealing?
On the darker side – they were cannibals –
weren't they? Think about it!
What happened to the rest? Who knows?
Nobody wrote it down – no history of
massacres here.

Perhaps they were saved by Christian charity
and blended in with the rest of us – or
maybe they died of natural causes
or just perished because they couldn't adapt.
The rest is mere hearsay – oral history –
words in the air!
Nothing on paper – so who remembers?
The Aborigines didn't count in numbers –
so why bother now?

Nobody recorded those other syllables in time –
full of sound and fury, punctuated by
blows, blood and screams.

But wasn't their blood red?
And didn't their loved ones cry?

Late in the twentieth century, with a population
of eighteen million the shootings of
thirty-five settlers went down in Australian history
as the Port Arthur Massacre prompting a
Prime Minister who denied Black massacres
to buy back the nation's firearms to minimise
the chance of another white one.

But wasn't their blood red too?
And didn't their loved ones still cry?
What is the colour of massacre?

Unearth
ALI COBBY ECKERMANN

let's dig up the soil and excavate the past
breathe life into the bodies of our ancestors
when movement stirs their bones
boomerangs will rattle in unison

it is not the noise of the poinciana
stirred by wind in its flaming limbs
the sound of the rising warriors echo
a people suppressed by dread

a hot wind whips up dust storms
we glimpse warriors in the mirage
in the future the petition will be everlasting
even when the language is changed

boomerang bones will return to memory
excavation holes are dug in our minds
the constant loss of breath is the legacy
there is blood on the truth

Domestic
NATALIE HARKIN

'The stories of Aboriginal women domestic servants cannot be told enough.
They illuminate a deeply-rooted racist facet of Australia's history. They tell of
the trials, tribulations and triumphs amidst the backdrop of oppression.'
— Jackie Huggins in *White Apron, Black Hands*, 1994.

'Girls of tender age and years are torn away from their parents ... and put to
service in an environment as near to slavery as it is possible to find.'
— Australian Aborigines Progressive Association, 1928.

The great need in dealing with the girls   of the [Point Pearce] mission
is that they be placed out   to domestic service   as they reach a
suitable age. There is no training and little for them to do   in a native
cottage home   and so many girls grow up   both useless and idol
Personally   I feel strongly that   voluntary effort in this direction   is
useless.   A compulsory systematic   placing of them out   is necessary
   Requests for the girls are often   received by me   and there would
be absolutely no difficulty   in finding situations for them.   They
become very capable   as domestic workers   especially at housework
and the laundry   I think any girl   so long as her health is right
can do domestic work.   The difficulty   with the natives   is that they
are lazy   I could do more with them   if obedience was enforced
but as it is   the parents   interfere so much.

Evidence: *South Australian Royal Commission on The Aborigines, 1913.*

The Ways of the Abo. Servant

By HELEN COLMAN.

I got her direct from a camp   some miles from here   and until she became used to things I had to tolerate the company   of her mother and younger sister   for a fortnight   [she] was then about 12 years (Jaykay 1926)   With all their drawbacks   however   the gins are more or less handy   about the place   though one needs tremendous patience to work them (Colman 1926)   Topsy has only been in my possession about six months   but I already feel   as if ten years   have been lifted from me   such is my peace of mind (CM 1925)   She loves washing   and is never happier   when her arms are deep   in soapsuds (Jaykay 1926) The children idolise her   she appears to them as   a real live gollywog and she is never tiring   in her games and devotions   to my babies (CM 1925)   They were both   fearsomely like baboons   even to their hairy faces and short thick necks   but as waitresses they could not have been better and their laundry work   was excellent (FPJ 1927)   Washing day was always more or less exciting one never knew   exactly what was going to happen   next (Colman 1926)

Aborigines Protection Board   1939
Committed to Institution   till 18 years
Charged   'Destitute'   Age 8

Apron Sorrow

apron-folds and pockets   keep secrets
pinned   tucked   hidden
they whisper   into linen-shadows
that flicker-float with the sun
hung
limp on the breeze they sway
a rhythmic
sorrow

She is very fond
of her own people
and is looking forward
to going home.

Took the Children Away

ARCHIE ROACH

This story's right, this story's true
I would not tell lies to you
Like the promises they did not keep
And how they fenced us in like sheep
Said to us, 'Come take our hand'
Sent us off to mission land
Taught us to read, to write and pray
Then they took the children away

Took the children away
The children away
Snatched from their mother's breast
Said, 'This is for the best'
Took them away

The welfare and the policeman
Said you've got to understand
We'll give to them what you can't give
Teach them how to really live
'Teach them how to live,' they said
Humiliated them instead
Taught them that and taught them this
And others taught them prejudice

You took the children away
The children away
Breaking their mothers' heart
Tearing us all apart
Took them away

One dark day on Framlingham
Came and didn't give a damn
My mother cried, 'Go get their dad'
He came running, fighting mad
Mother's tears were falling down
Dad shaped up and stood his ground
He said, 'You touch my kids and you fight me'
And they took us from our family

Took us away
They took us away
Snatched from our mother's breast
Said this was for the best
Took us away

Told us what to do and say
Told us all the white man's ways
Then they split us up again
And gave us gifts to ease the pain
Sent us off to foster homes
As we grew up we felt alone
'Cause we were acting white
Yet feeling black
One sweet day all the children came back

The children came back
The children came back
Back where their hearts grow strong
Back where they all belong
The children came back

Said the children came back
The children came back
Back where they understand
Back to their mother's land
The children came back

Back to their mother
Back to their father
Back to their sister
Back to their brother
Back to their people
Back to their land

All the children came back
The children came back
The children came back
Yes I came back

The Children Came Back
BRIGGS (FT. GURRUMUL YUNUPINGU)

I'm Fitzroy where the stars be
I'm Wanganeen in '93
I'm Mundine. I'm Cathy Free-
Man, that fire inside-a-me
I'm Adam Goodes, and Adam should
Be applauded when he stand up
You can look to us when that time stop
I'm Patty Mills with the last shot

I'm Gurrumul, I'm Archie
I'm everything that you ask me
I'm everything that you can't be
I'm the dead heart's, heart beat

    The children came back
    The children came back
    Back where their hearts grow strong,
        back where they all belong
    The children came back

I'm Doug Nicholls, I'm Jimmy Little
With a royal telephone
I'm the world champ in '68
Boy I'm Lionel Rose

I'm William Cooper, I take a stand
When no one even knows
I'm the walk off, I'm the sound of
The children coming home

Boy I'm Gurrumul, I'm Archie
I'm everything that you ask me
I'm everything that you can't be
I'm the dead hearts, heart beat

    The children came back
    The children came back
    Back where their hearts grow strong,
       back where they all belong
    The children came back

Let me take it home, I'm Rumba
I'm the sand hills on Cummera
I'm Les Briggs, I'm Paul Briggs
I'm Uncle Ringo with all them kids
I'm Uncle Buddy, everybody loves me
Ain't none below, ain't none above me
I'm the carvings outta every scar tree
I'm those flats that birthed Archie
Now Mr Abbott, think about that
Me and you we feel the same
That might sound strange, I'm just sayin'
We both unsettled when the boats came

I'm Gurrumul, I'm Archie
I'm everything that you ask me
I'm everything that you can't be
I'm the dead hearts, heart beat

    The children came back
    The children came back
    Back where their hearts grow strong,
        back where they all belong
    The children came back

    The children came back
    The children came back
    Back where they understand,
        back to their mothers' land
    The children came back

    The children came back
    The children came back
    Back where their hearts grow strong,
        back where they all belong
    The children came back

Yúya Karrabúrra (Fire Is Burning)

ALICE EATHER

I'm standing by this fire
The embers smoking
The ashes glowing
The coals weighing us down
The youth are buried in the rubble
My eyes are burning
And through my nostrils
The smoke is stirring
I breathe it in

Yúya Karrabúrra

I wear a ship on my wrist
That shows my blood comes from convicts
On the Second Fleet
My fathers' forefathers came
Whipped beaten and bound in chains
The dark tone in my skin
The brown in my eyes
Sunset to sunrise
My Wúrnal mother's side
My Kíkka who grew up in a dugout canoe
In her womb is where my consciousness grew

Yúya Karrabúrra

I walk between these two worlds
A split life
Split skin
Split tongue
Split kin
Everyday these worlds collide
And I'm living and breathing
This story of black and white

Sitting in the middle of this collision
My mission is to bring
Two divided worlds to sit beside this fire
And listen
Through this skin I know where I belong
It is both my centre
And my division

Yúya Karrabúrra

My ancestors dance in the stars
And their tongues are in the flames
And they tell me:
You have to keep the fire alive
Between the black and the white
There's a story waiting to be spoken

In every life
There's a spirit waiting to be woken
Now I'm looking at you
With stars in my eyes

And my tongue is burning flames
And I say

Yúya Karrabúrra

The sacred songs are still being sung
But the words are slowly fading
The distant cries I'm hearing
Are the mothers burying their babies
The Elders are standing strong
But the ground beneath them is breaking

Yúya Karrabúrra

Now I welcome you to sit beside my fire
I'm allowing you to digest my confusion
I will not point my finger and blame
Cause when we start blaming each other
We make no room for changing each other

We've got to keep this fire burning
With ash on our feet and coal in our hands
Teach Barra-rodjibba
All them young ones how to live side by side
Cause tomorrow when the sun rises
And our fires have gone quiet
They will be the ones to reignite it

Yúya Karrabúrra

These flames
Us
Will be their guidance

Bilya Kep
DEBORAH DOORLAK L. MOODY

Bilya Kep

Nitja ngulla bilya-kep korrliny
Ngangk yirra yaaginy,
Shimmering silver in the morning
Koorliny down through the bilya
in the deep moorn kep.

Bending, winding koorliny in straight lines
around corners bokadja.
Baalap waanginy in the dreamtime
He created the bilya kep.

Maaman God baal yirra yaaginy
over the deep moorn kep.
Maaman God baal waanginy,
separate the boodja and the kep.

The deep moorn kep
koorliny bokadja.
Ngulla maaman God
baal the creator
of the boodja and
the deep moorn kep.

Black Woman
RUBY LANGFORD GINIBI

I am every black woman who's ever been loved. I am every black woman who's been serenaded by a guitar on a starry night. I am every black woman who's ever been betrayed by a selfish lover. I am every black woman who's given birth to loved children. I am every black woman who's had to work on fence lines to raise them too! I am every black woman who's hungered after truth! I am every black woman who's ever-carted water buckets on yokes, to fill a forty-four gallon drum, for drinkin', washin', and cookin' purposes. I am every black woman, who's had a son, or husband jailed! I am every black woman who's had iron doors slammed shut, going to visit them too! I am every black woman who's struggled to raise a fine. I am every black woman who has survived this calamity called life, in this multicultural Australia.

A Letter to the Shade of Charles Darwin
JACK DAVIS

We sincerely wish to thank you
for the assistance you have unwittingly given us
in the occupation of this continent
It is better far better that we
that we the intelligent and superior ones
were able to enlighten and lighten the burden of those poor
miserable halfstarved
bottlenosed caricatures
of humanity who aimlessly wandered this land
for centuries before our arrival
It was better far better that we
that we led them out of barbarism
into the era of Christendom by baptising
bibling blanketing and clothing them
As a small token of gratitude
for we are grateful in being able to assist you
and your colleagues we are forwarding to you
The heads of Pomawoy and Yagan
which I believe are two of the purest specimens
of skulls of brute man
ever to leave our shores
Caucasian man has much to thank you for
in propounding the laws of selectivity
In relation to Homo Erectus
in Australia and beyond

Yours faithfully
Sylvester Squatter

PS   My friends and I
will send you further specimens
when they come to hand
S.S.

**'Despite what Dorothea has said
about the sun scorched land'**

– Kevin Gilbert, 'The New True Anthem'

Too Little, Too Much
EVELYN ARALUEN

'I call on you to anticipate nothing from Indigenous poetry, but brace for everything.'

– Alison Whittaker

Aboriginal poetics have always existed. Or, at least, they fulfil every sense of always that we have access to: yaburuhma, the kind of eternal that spirals out a constant across time and space; forever, the kind of promise we make to spread between every time. Since the land, since the land made us shape, since the land gave us voice, since we had learned enough to inscribe it back, since we took up tools tossed here by the uninvited. We sing it back as it is sung back to us in every bird song, every branch ache, every wave heave. The form has changed, as have we, but the songlines still hum in the soil while we read and write upon it.

Aboriginal poetics have always been caught within the gaze of too little, too much.

After the publication of *We Are Going* (1964), critics slandered Oodgeroo Noonuccal's verses as too radical, more propaganda than poetry. Some speculated whether she had written them at all. In 1973, Ruth Doobov wrote of *My People* (1970), a collection dedicated to those fighting for treaty, that Noonuccal 'is not in a position to have a very sensitive appreciation of European verse rhythms, but at the same time she cannot use the structure and techniques of the poetry of her Aboriginal ancestors.' Despite the commercial and cultural success Oodgeroo Noonuccal's work attracted within and beyond the nation, the poems of protest, remembrance and celebration she performed on the shores of her beloved Minjerribah, and for the Federal Council for the Advancement of Aborigines and Torres Strait Islanders alike, articulated something unsettling in white Australian literary culture. A thing wronged. She was curated and contained, like the municipal gum she so forlornly looked upon: *O fellow citizen, / What have they done to us?*

Although little commercial opportunity was afforded to Aboriginal poets in the following decades, writers such as Kevin Gilbert and Lionel Fogarty published and performed in every available space. They were met with varying levels of recognition and respect from a conservative settler-colonial literary audience eager to distance the protest from the poetry. Gilbert renounced his first collection *End of Dream-Time* in 1971, after his editor altered the meaning of the work beyond recognition. 'The New True Anthem' is one of Gilbert's many poems that critique the hypocrisy of the Australian literary and cultural imaginary. Gilbert's voice speaks to the superficial attempt of a shallow literary nationalism to stake itself on a fetishised landscape in the context of a dwindling British empire. He juxtaposes this facile romanticism against the hypocrisy of Australian authors turning their backs on the blood spilt to dispossess its rightful custodians:

Despite what Dorothea has said
about the sun scorched land
you've never really loved her
nor sought to make her grand

Fogarty writes of Gilbert and Noonuccal as callers to collaboration: a linguistic resistance to the great venom, the great vernacular against which black writing is performed and energised in communal acts of voice and inscriptions, reminding us how ancestors are made. *Please Oodgeroo Noonuccal and Mr Kevin Gilbert pregnant us again, / I all in dawns of the night's day's writer's futures.* Our legacies become futures, written from and for *anywhere.*

Aboriginal poetry is not obliged to respond to the colonial canon, but in this suite we see the concentration of power and perception that Aboriginal voices bring to the institutions and textures of Australian literature's cultural dominance. Alison Whittaker's 'Many Girls White Linen' peels back the fine dressings and class signifiers concealing structures of violence, exploitation and erasure, the stories rendered spectral and unspoken when later plaques will mark this war. Sam Wagan Watson calls up these ghosts for the hunt in 'The Grounding Sentence', shooting down the icons of colonial appropriation from Country scarred by their brandings. Oscillating between grief and rage, despair and warning, inertia wields itself refusing and unreadable:

I have hunted for trophies of my own and fallen into the
snares of what the invader prides most of all, and that is

the ability to turn blood against blood. There's nothing
noble about becoming a savage in the despair of your own
people … I am the most ignorant savage of them all …
I cannot interpret the words of my Dreaming.

Lorna Munro's 'YILAALU – BU-GADI (Once Upon a Time in the Bay of Gadi)' subverts Eurowestern conventions of taxonomy and anthropology through a choral performance of the spatiality of culture. Where modernity demands the binary differentiation of subject and object, Munro's voice circles the presences and artefacts of culture, arriving at precept and law through that attention, staging honest dialogue with Country to disperse the projected definitions and classifications inscribed on it from above.

As Penny van Toorn has argued, European writing entered Aboriginal life as a vehicle of governmentality and control, and as such will always be marked with these violences. But these poets build as much as they break. The poems of this suite, this anthology, this movement of black poets speaking into the always, is politically necessitated, but never constrained by its context. In our voices, the *great venom* of the *great vernacular* Fogarty witnesses can be made deft and tender.

It's in the gleeful making-visible of materiality in Elizabeth Hodgson's 'Boots': *I love the feel of the press of the leather against / my feet tucked snugly inside my boots as the shoe-shine man / works at the leather.*

The heady hilarity of new black everydays in the Diwurruwurru group's 'Millad Mob Da Best!': *an dey bin singin us mob bullocky dreamin song / day bin learnin us mob / for to sing im an everyone deadly safe.*

It smiles back in the nervous flirtation of Alf Taylor's 'Moorditj Yorgah': *Um gonna get off dis gerbah an' gunja / an' show you what a moorditj man I can be / an' gib you all da lub dat I can / but kurndarnj choo um shame.*

Today the new tensions in Australian and global Indigenous poetics emerge less from accusations of simplicity – what Driftpile Cree Nation poet Billy-Ray Belcourt describes as a word to 'lay me flat on the floor of the world' – and more from anxious cultivations of authenticity in forms and structures that are not yet ready for the fullness of our histories. As black poets, our editorial devices must often negotiate those too littles and too muches that still try to frame the place of our languages in verse. The tension between them operates as a closure:

'Can you cut back some of the language? It trips up the reader and no-one is going to know what you're saying.'

'I'd love if you could use some more of language. Is there an Aboriginal word for tree you could use here?'

There are interesting questions to ask of Aboriginal poetics, and then there are constraining ones. Noonuccal's longtime friend and collaborator Judith Wright observed this in 1988, asking: 'Do we go on talking from our critical heights, as though our standards are necessarily to be accepted even by those who have no cause to thank us for them?' Speaking with and to Aboriginal poetry, there's so much more to be said about what we're doing, than what we are not.

We are always writing around the implied subalternity of Aboriginal poets writing in English. These poems demonstrate that there's fun to be had in satirising the transplanted cadence of Anglo-Saxon verse through fragmentation and irony, straining and interrogating the positionality of settler-colonial poeticism. None of these poems leave English, or the structures it has projected over our Country, unscathed. Across the thematics of temporality, Dreaming, custodianship and love, these poems juxtapose every afterlife of Eurowestern verse imported here off the tall ships against the perpetuity of Culture. We invent new forms: post-canonical, land-centric, kinship-connective, everyday-assertive. As poets we try things on for size, and discard that which cannot speak us. As Fogarty reminds us, Aboriginal poetry is here: *Liberating words where we have half the times don't need words.*

These poems push, comforted in the knowledge that our words are more important than the grammars that restrain them. They play, knowing that none of these games are departures from the land which gave us our first languages: even as we invent new forms, we strive towards the textures and memories of those languages.

Aboriginal poetics always have, and always will be here – extending the land and waters into air. Our poetries will grow as we grow, as we remember and return. Our words bear with them more than scholars like myself know what to do with them. They speak to the kind of always that isn't threatened by worlds spinning on around it.

The Grounding Sentence

SAMUEL WAGAN WATSON

'On Friday, Rockhampton Magistrates Court heard that [a male], 17, had been driving around with an air gun looking to "shoot an Aboriginal person" on Australia Day ...'
    – 'Stung teen shot in back', *The Sunday Mail*, 29 January 2006

i

It has been an eternity of dispersal. Knowledge, secret and sacred ... my people have become the most written about Indigenous nations of the world ... but are any of those words valuable? The world my children inherit is a scattered plain; the earth is flat and often void of the echoes of their elders. For too long I have listened to the wind as it is spoken by passing semitrailers and luxury cars. For too long I have complacently existed on these killing fields and built a house of straw in the down-wind of the enemy. My ancestors' tongues are sealed and delivered trophies on the shelves of the invaders' sterile museums ... for too long I have permitted the hunter inside of me to become the hunted.

Australians all let us rejoice, for we are young and free ...

ii.

From the southern banks of the Brisbane River my Mununjali
blood flows south. My Birri-Gubba blood is far in the north,
on the Dawson River, another river, another world away.
Worlds swept with the changing winds of successive hunting
regulations and administrations. From the moment we are
born we are taught who we are and where we cannot go, but
to be out of range is the safest place to be, no matter where
your blood flows. Open game and fair game are two hearts of
darkness that beat as one. The skin of the country is branded
deep with crosshairs and warning signs.

> *A sunburnt country*
> *land of extreme prejudice*
> *advance Australia where?*

iii.

I have hunted for trophies of my own and fallen into the
snares of what the invader prides most of all, and that is
the ability to turn blood against blood. There's nothing
noble about becoming a savage in the despair of your own
people ... I am the most ignorant savage of them all ...
I cannot interpret the words of my Dreaming.

I cannot fly straight
a reluctant boomerang
my grounding sentence

Mununjali refers to my nan's tribe in the Beaudesert region.
Birri Gubba refers to my pop's tribe on the central Queensland coast.

Caused Us To Be Collaborator

LIONEL FOGARTY

(Anywhere, 2013-06-29)

Their minds in times is what rhymes
We see their words beyond any acceptable meaning
And this is how we express their Dreaming

Because a Black man woman cool done it,
   For all first and human.
Written on paper for the poorest
Wrote on bark for the richest
Because International 1920 Minjerriba she's readopted.
Because intentional Wiradjuri mind he educator,
   Of body's pains for spirit higher educating.
A poetic kill of those non protest writers,
Even oiling the dramatist idea after death to the up coming.
Because this woman man contributing never fades,
A house in his name must be given as foundations abilities.
Never we pay injustices by his words,
We say the price of patriot's lives out of the pages he gave, as
   he's legend.
Australians need to know, survival by Black writers who talk
   read in the pickers' sovereignty hits the heart to love the
   minds to fight rich bug gars of edged level demands.
The healing of national treasures,
Don't stay on the fringes.
So people's poets think for his positive process.

So main man Mr Gilbert is the messages for our baby's writer's
     cultural matrix.
Streams of influence are seen read in those who don't know the
     black man woman writing even when it touches when not
     there, hey?
Because ghosts are not alive, but the voice off the paper
     reconciliation our negotiation to answers.
Foisted simply power giving us intelligentsia,
Who can galvanisation the call to political actions?
Repetition of the majority written forms is broken by
     provided powers.
Because the white man cannot write, means he's cannot speak
     for the introduce Black from jails.
Let alone repeat the forces of how we must write.
Here Mr Gilbert boarded all our widespread solutions.
Only if they have listen to him may he would be dead or alive.
Treaty reference is legislative frames in occurred lifetime position.
Yet the necessary times declare of plague in the affairs are
     Indigenous condemnation of their dimension writers.
Being the playwright's solitary vision gave us aspirate facts to
     give criticism of Governments present.
Strike appeal intervened epilogue in no debate but outcomes
     and say just because he absence is ours to rethink refight
     and rewrite.
I witness this great venom,
I withstand this great vernacular,
     the kind of fashion glorious of our prides.
Liberating words where we have half the times don't need words.

A resists on evil by enshrines of poems so immortal that's all
   our legendary never needs to keep on quest justice, but to
   live its determination without convictions.
The dictum by those written dead poets are to oppress terror
   by the white man's laws.
Personal becomes echo of authentic grass-roots politeness,
Still shows to have peace must protest
Still shows to have apology must not lay down our dead who
   fought for the refusals still our peoples do.
I witness spiritual reflect of great experiences in they are apart of
   all our ultimately writer fighters even lovers of the sentences
   to go on forever.
Perform our unions to instil Aboriginal in years to come still
   greater authors,
Oodgeroo Noonuccal, Mr Gilbert.
He and she had a white side,
Knowing get their words out to clean up the untrue written
   poetry of politics.
They lived near white foe but never stole their ideas or rid to
   get rips.
They were common but differ in how to pawn the way over and
   around Miggloo brains.
They even had a good go at their own kinds.
Anyways every out massacres to lectures was to shame the
   systems and make human righties loves be a thing of essential.
The original most in heartlands cannot be a new Australian spirits
   for the original made us richer on the steel worlds forecasts.
Now new ones hype on their medias communicate for that magic
   formulate.

So just because we will never change the way they wrote, we can
 learn look and sit for the teachings.
Please Oodgeroo Noonuccal and Mr Kevin Gilbert pregnant
 us again,
I all in dawns of the night's day's writer's futures.
Because us writers arts can do it all for all thanks and thanks again
Call us the collaborators of their books ...

Connoisseur
LIONEL FOGARTY
(Merton, Victoria, Sunday, 2013-05-12)

They are excursionist on our culture
We are in a degree of velocity
You recoil in a ricochet of
Love to retroactive beliefs
Was satellite progressive?
Tractions stop you'll
Find our gravity
Being convergence to your
Admissions is what influxes
Our distillations.
This discharge baths in bright
Prostrated bloodiness
And our depressions are
Shortcoming in transmission
And our rotation turns to a
Plunging dizzy cyclone
We are spirits of levity
This globe wide by massive
Textures are becoming a
Friction with nature
At the delta we die
At the peninsula we live
Your vaporisation of lives
Won't corroborate within us
They dogmatise the blackfella
And upshot miscalculations

Even presumptions are made
In a scepticism way
Our communications is to our Murris
Our doctrine is to our Murris
Our faith or professions is to Murris
But your doubt is yet a white
Man's discredit
But you assent knowledge
Of philosophy theory and encyclopaedia
For higher blackfellas to proficiency
Well these intellectual faculties
Are unsophisticated to our Murri
Imagined realistic minds
They are substantiated precision over
Our veritable culture Murri
Just exactitude illiterate maniac scholars.

Darkinjung Burning
LUKE PATTERSON

begin with a circle facing a fire aunty
lit under the blinking pink and kindle
dawn moon nevertheless still splashing
in the breeze rest handfuls of striplet
sprigs moiety-up arc an interspecies
intimacy until a dozen landscapes egress
with a eucalyptus lungful and the supernatural
appear commonsense in tempered embers
this is not a mourning poem you see
places are totemic uncle dips bottlebrush
dew admits life begins with yellowbelly

*

untroubled chuckle in gestures
the way the land-owner cites edible plants
surveys the shape the colour of eyes
a course of native spices peppers cosmopolitan
phenotypes he smokes a pipe with a timber
pulse and jokes how he plundered through
Dark Emu in a week and thanks god for the
seasons urging to get on with business
eat biscuits wait for the wind to calm
sheepish hawks circle thermal pockets
birdsong warms the valley lips

*

didn't fall from our mother's clacker
with a pair of clapsticks in our hands aunty
calls a tenure of love a labor of warmth for light
for ceremony for hardening the point spearhead
the facts face the leviathan that chokes
the undergrowth and wraps its brambled body
around the roots untouched scales a forsaken
gallery this toothache country uncle growls years
of gub-abo leaf litter over his shoulders
letting in a little peace of sky clearing
the air which left untended is prone to ignition

*

auntie yawns two-stepping with a willywagtail
driptorch in her hand tilts yolk from an egg
little min-min ooze out dance fiddle-footed
nothing cataclysmic no holocenic genocide
no pyretic extinction just a fizz seeds pop tickle
lick with a pitch and chimerical taste of species
in cahoots no war but a wash of living soot no
breakneck rush but simply slips down the slope
flush like a droplet down the wrist a murmuration
of carapaces and critters scurrying up trunks
a breath before a din no woodwind lakestorm
no brouhaha only the heartstrings the burning
dipthong unbuttoning years of flora and flesh
lost on the logophile we walk and talk on a hotbed
of rolling bio-semiosis side-by-side a wandering
phantonym in mnemonic attires cool to the touch
and calm as wallabies watching in the distance

Many Girls White Linen
ALISON WHITTAKER

no mist no mystery
no hanging rock only

many girls white linen
men with guns and
harsher things white women
amongst gums white linen
starch'er things later plaques
will mark this war
nails peeling back floor
scrubbing back blak chores
white luxe hangnails hanging
more than nails while
no palm glowing paler

later plaques will mark
this sick linen's rotten
cotton genes later plaques
will track the try
to bleed lineage dry

its banks now flood
a new ancestor, Ordeal,
plaits this our blood

if evil is banal
how more boring is

suffering evil two bloodlines
from it how more
raw rousing horrifying is
the plaque that marks
something else rolling on
from this place a
roll of white linen
dropped on slight incline
amongst gums collecting grit
where blak girls hang
nails hang out picking
them hangnails

Municipal Gum
OODGEROO NOONUCCAL

Gumtree in the city street,
Hard bitumen around your feet,
Rather you should be
In the cool world of leafy forest halls
And wild bird calls
Here you seems to me
Like that poor cart-horse
Castrated, broken, a thing wronged,
Strapped and buckled, its hell prolonged,
Whose hung head and listless mien express
Its hopelessness.
Municipal gum, it is dolorous
To see you thus
Set in your black grass of bitumen —
O fellow citizen,
What have they done to us?

Millad Mob Da Best!
DIWURRUWURRU (WITH PHILLIP HALL)

For Patsy Shadforth & Borroloola's kids

We likem dat Borroloola Rodeo
my kardu im gotta ridem dat big one bullocky
dat bull im jump really really high
im buck too much, makem dirt thunderin dust-burst
an big mob snot grunt from im nose
an dat bullocky im got wide open bash ya eyes
an im body like bullet train growlin dat mad one crowd
so kardu he hang on very very tight for millad mob
an e bin win dat big one trophy
makem all so proud a hallelulah
saviour one of all dem deadly dagger rides

wen do gate crack open my big one buja come crashin
out on gunfired screwed-up muscle ngabaya of a horse
come on buja, hang on
dat big one horse, e bin bash, buck an sling
wid so much hate an really really high
buja bin hold on cowboy roped on tight
dat horse e bin make biggest mob blackfulla roar
like barri barri burst but buja bin ride on an on an on
e bin win big pack money an millad mob all so teary proud

we bin get up an hab-im gooda one feed
us mob excited rowdy
no one bare foot on tis shiny one best of day
us mob all cowboy boot, bull hide hat, silky showoff shirt,
trouser an chaps wid mad one colour of fringe an fray
we bin jumin the mudika
an we bin go race race rodeo ground
mimmi an kukudi bin come too
an dey bin singin us mob bullocky dreamin song
day bin learnin us mob
for to sing im an everyone deadly safe
we like learn for singin us mob song
for ceremony, culture, land an law
millad mob strong in dat rodeo an in dreamin us proud

Barri Barri is Indigenous Language in the Gulf region of Northern Australia for 'shooting star'.

Buja is Kriol in the Gulf region of Northern Australia for 'brother'.

Kardu is Indigenous Language in the Gulf region of Northern Australia for 'uncle'.

Kujika is Indigenous Language in the Gulf region of Northern Australia for Songlines; Indigenous Country 'beats with the rhythm' of Kujika.

Kukudi is Indigenous Language in the Gulf region of Northern Australia for 'nana' or grandmother, on your mother's side.

Millad is Kriol in the Gulf region of Northern Australia for the first person plural pronoun: we, us, our.

Mimi is Indigenous Language in the Gulf region of Northern Australia for 'pop' or grandfather, on your mother's side.

Mudika is Kriol in the Gulf region of Northern Australia for 'motorcar'.

Ngabaya is Indigenous Language in the Gulf region of Northern Australia for 'ghost' or 'spirit'.

YILAALU – BU-GADI
(Once Upon a Time in the Bay of Gadi)
LORNA MUNRO

MELALEUCA

YURALI (eucalyptus)

PAPERBARK

KURRAJONG

MOTHER TONGUE WILL ALWAYS GUIDE YOU
HOME BY SONG

TALLAWOLADAH

WHITE CLAY

MENS BUSINESS

WUCUNMUGULLY

THE LAY OF THIS LAND, IF YOU CARE TO LISTEN
WILL TELL ITS EXCLUSIVE STORY

YIILINHI

RED CLAY

MULGUN

JUBAGULLY

THIS TERRAIN EVOLVED OVER MANY EONS AND
IN A RAMBUNCTIOUS FLURRY

DUGONG

LEATHER JACKET

SALMON

JOHN DORY

ANCIENT WATER WAYS IN ALL THEIR GLORY

PIRRAMA

BA-ING-HOE

MEL MEL

WARRUNG

ART, SWIMMING, DANCING AND CONTEST
REGIMENTED FUN

BARRA (fish hook)

BARANI (yesterday)

BADU (water)

BARRABUGU (today)

MANY VANTAGE POINTS TO BE DIRECTED TO

KANGAROO

BADABARANG

DINGU

ENDLESS RITES OF PASSAGE TO CEREMONIOUSLY
PASS THROUGH

SHELLS

SCARS

SWEET SMELLS

A YOUNG GADIGALEON WOULD KNOW ALL TOO
WELL

KADAICHA

OILS

MEDICINE MAN

TEA-TREE FOR YOUR WOUNDS WHEN HEALTH
ISN'T SO SWELL

GAWURA DREAMING

SALT WATER

GARRI GARRANG

THE OCEAN OPENS ITS EMBRACE LIKE AN OLD
FRIEND

NOWEY

GUNYA

MARRANG

TIME AND PLACE TRANSCEND

Moorditj Yorgah

ALF TAYLOR

You are a cruel deadly moorditj yorgah an' um marrdong for you
but um just a wintjarren Nyoongar man
Um gonna try and get off diss gerbah an' gunja
an' be a cruel deadly moorditj Nyoongar man
You are indeed a truly deadly solid moorditj yorgah
an' um jerrepjing something wicked for you
but um just a wintjarren Nyoongar man.
Um gonna get off diss gerbah an' gunja
an' show you what a moorditj man I can be
an' gib you all da lub dat I can
but kurndarnj choo um shame.

The New True Anthem

KEVIN GILBERT

Despite what Dorothea has said
about the sun scorched land
you've never really loved her
nor sought to make her grand
you pollute all the rivers
and litter every road
your barbaric graffiti
cut scars where tall trees grow
the beaches and the mountains
are covered with your shame
injustice rules supremely
despite your claims to fame
the mud polluted rivers
are fenced off from the gaze
of travellers and the thirsty
for foreign hooves to graze
a tyranny now rules your soul
to your own image blind
a callousness and uncouth ways
now hallmarks of your kind
Australia oh Australia
you could stand proud and free
we weep in bitter anguish
at your hate and tyranny
the scarred black bodies writhing
humanity locked in chains
land theft and racial murder

you boast on of your gains
in woodchip and uranium
the anguished death you spread
will leave the children of the land
a heritage that's dead
Australia oh Australia
you could stand tall and free
we weep in bitter anguish
at your hate and tyranny.

Boots
ELIZABETH HODGSON

I have an obsession with polished boots
and walk the streets looking for a shoe-shine man
slip my hand into my overcoat pocket
feel for a pound coin
slide onto a wooden seat,
or a vinyl stool
polished free of charge
by many and varied arses
sliding backwards and forth across its roundness
worn down
in the front, sloping gently forward.
An old stool
easier to push back into.

I climbed on one and slid straight back off
the shoe-shine man catching me,
he got used to catching his customers.
I love the feel of the press of the leather against
my feet tucked snugly inside my boots as the shoe-shine
    man
works at the leather,
his brush moving quickly
ch-ch-ch-ch-ch-ch-ch
across, around and over my boots.

'I say rage and dreaming'

— Evelyn Araluen, 'Dropbear Poetics'

Bleat Beneath a Blanket
BRUCE PASCOE

I often think of the vision of the Old People in constructing our culture on such egalitarian and environmentally loving principles – but that then leads to being overwhelmed by the devastation of soul they must have experienced when the Invaders so wilfully destroyed that social design.

Imagine living in a world where people in colder climates built substantial houses in which they could stand upright and draw on the walls and ceiling. Houses were found all over the country, some accommodating over fifty people; one was used as a mess hall for the sailors of a ship. How did the owners feel watching others carouse beneath their civil roof. All the houses reflected the taste of the owners. It was an aesthetic world.

Imagine eating the harvest of vegetables and grains which were domesticated by your ancestors. Your people invented aquaculture, art, bread and … society. We will soon be allowed to talk about Australia having the oldest villages on earth and therefore having invented society.

Does it rankle that we have to wait so that a white university allows that information to be released? Does it gnaw at your spirit that we can't comment on an incredible example of plant cultivation until *Nature* has published it first?

This is still a colonised world.

That is a burr in the britches compared to how the Old People must have felt when they saw sheep eating their crops, cattle shitting on the sacred lagoon, men being shot, women being raped, and the subtle fabric of the lore being unravelled bit by bit over the long agonising days of the rest of their lives. The pain, the indignity, the sorrow, the humiliation, the frustration that white people were deaf and blind to the beautiful planning of a culture over 120,000 years old.

I believe that sentiment is expressed in Joel Davison's poem 'Ngayrayagal Didjurigur (Soon Enough)'.

> *Wiribay Dagura*
> *Worn out and cold*
> *Gadi wari*
> *Under and away*
> *Ngarrawan biyal*
> *Distant and no where*
>
> *Gunamabami ngyini*
> *You will set yourself alight again*
> *Manabami ngyini*
> *You will collect yourself again*
> *Nabami ngyini*
> *You will see yourself again*
> *Ngyinila*
> *You must*

The desolation felt by those old philosophers must have been inexpressible. The awful pain of their distress made the earth quake and that quaking reverberates with us still – we shudder and moan – and, unable to unseat the conqueror, our anger sometimes turns on our own, the impotent striking of frustration and hurt.

How can we honour the Old People's grand strategy for lasting peace if we turn on each other?

Poetry.

Is that archaic form of expression enough? Are there enough readers left to make it more than a bleat beneath a blanket? Do we use it to hurt those who have hurt us or can we use it to sew up the old possum skin of restraint and civility?

Perhaps Charmaine Papertalk Green has an answer in 'Honey to Lips Bottlebrush'.

> *Dance ground feet sand reunite connect*
> *Still wind still ancestors come to visit*
> *Gentle kiss giving to young spirits*
> *Reassuring for the onward journey*
> *Right here on this land right here*

I admire the spirit because plenty of times my words have been acid-etched steel. I feel the pain and anger of Evelyn Araluen in 'Dropbear Poetics'.

> *Waagan says use heart*
> *but I am rage and dreaming*

> *at the gloss green palm fronds*
> *of this gentry aestheantique*
> > *all this potplanting in our sovereignty*
> > *a garden for you to swallow speak our blood*

I know that anger. I have used it and mostly hurt myself.

Romaine Morton says it best in 'Are You Beautiful Today?'

> *could you take*
> *conversations about jail and suicide*
> *and make it as though*
> *you were saying*
> *one lump*
> *or*
> *two,*

Australia is comfortable in its ignorance of the Aboriginal past and present – at best a kindly patronage, allowing illness, unemployment and incarceration as if they are the dying fish in rivers robbed of water by billionaire cotton farmers, a maths too difficult for an Australian to compute. Will our words be enough to battle the tea-cosy nature of Australian comfort?

Well, our people have always sung in verse: we named a bend in the river Kardinia after the first rays of the morning sun; we named a hill Bellawein which may mean either a view from where the water sparkles like fire or perhaps leaning on our elbow by the fire or a more subtle blend of the two, but whoever created the expression was a poet and perhaps a poet long before Europe had chanced upon the idea of aesthetic language.

We are the wordsmiths of the world; we spoke seven to ten languages and used long and complex words in all of them to explain long and complex philosophical statements. We should not apologise for being good with words and their use – it is our heritage.

The Boorong clan of the Wergaia at Lake Tyrell used the flat surface of the lake as a mirror to view and fathom the stars and the universe. Think of that image: a people gathered about a lake and looking down to contemplate the night sky. It is the instinct of the poet, the habit of a philosophical spirit. A million Chinese visitors go there every year because they are interested in philosophy, but Australians couldn't point to it on a map.

See how easily I slipped into spleen? Where was my calm, where was my generosity?

Eroded and crippled by indifference – that's where. And yet the ancestors urge us toward patience and peace, for both were the bedrock of the lore. I try – and I see my brothers and sisters try – to overcome the deepest bruise to the brain.

I admire them their energy but wonder if our words will be enough?

The ancestors of course would keep wording, even to the deaf.

Ngayrayagal Didjurigur (Soon Enough)

JOEL DAVISON

Ngayrayagal didjurigur
Soon enough
Soon enough

Birragu gudjibi
Hollow and decayed
Wurral gujimay
Sluggish and blinded
Wiribay dagura
Worn out and cold

Dudbadjami
You concealed yourself
Nanga
Sleepy
Wulumi Birragu gudjibi
Worse, hollow and decayed

Manuwi Buwabili
Feet buried
Damuna
Refusing
Bulwurra yiningma
Gaze, allowed to fall
Bemulguwiya
Only grit
Wulumi Wurral Gujimay
Worse, sluggish and blinded

Wiribay dagura
Worn out and cold
Gadi wari
Under and away
Ngarrawan biyal
Distant and nowhere

Gunamabami ngyini
You will set yourself alight again
Manabami ngyini
You will collect yourself again
Nabami ngyini
You will see yourself again
Ngyinila
You must

Djarradjarrabawawi
They will lean on you
Nababami muru
You will see the path
Walamami
You will return
Munurubuni
Do not forget
Ngyinila
You must

Expert
ELLEN VAN NEERVEN

Poor me
don't know how it happened
think I got
a non-Indigenous girlfriend
who thinks she's an expert
don't know how she's got her expertise
think I'm the first one she's met
yet
she tells me I'm closed to other sides of the debate
that she has the answers because she saw a television ad
for Recognition
and though most Indigenous Australians are opposed
she says it's for our good
talks about drunks and sexual abuse 'up north'
devalues my own knowledge (too urban)
and anything I get from black media
(not the whole truth
I wouldn't trust it)
she likes to argue when she's had a few
13 times more
her voice loud
(87%) of intimate partner homicides
fresh tears on my face
involving Indigenous people, are alcohol related
she's drunk, I tell the booliman
still shaking. Sitting on the steps.
no, I haven't had any

won't let her forget this statistic
tonight it's her
in the paddy wagon

Dropbear Poetics
EVELYN ARALUEN

      Tiddalik say
I'm such great thirst
I will drain the land
and drag my big fat belly
across the empty sea

      Bunyip say
I'm gonna gobble you up
if you step waters where I sleep
and with wet claws I will snatch
your spine and ankles to fill them
                with stain and stench

      what the Mopoke say
don't need saying
if you grown up under his eyes

now here's the part
you write Black Snake down
for a dilly of national flair
      true god you don't know how wild I'm gonna be
      to every fucking postmod blinky bill
      tryna crack open my country
      mining in metaphors
      for that place you felt *felt* you
           somewhere in
           the Royal National

Waagan says use heart
but I am rage and dreaming
at the gloss green palm fronds
of this gentry aestheantique
     all this potplanting in our sovereignty
     a garden for you to swallow speak our blood

if you're taking that talk
you gotta scrape it from my schoolhouse walls
filter gollywog ashtray snugglepot kitsch
into your pastoral deconstruct
     fill four'n twenty pies
     with artisan magpies
     if you sever their heads
     you can wear them to the doof

I say rage and dreaming
for making liar the lyrebird
for making mimetic
the power   Baiami gave
when Ribbon's mischief swallowed first life
     ochre dust
     creation breath
     ancestor song

we aren't here
     to hear you poem
you do wrong   you get wrong
you get
gobbled up

Honey to Lips Bottlebrush
CHARMAINE PAPERTALK GREEN

Young teachings perched on Walkaway hill
Space reclaiming decolonising respacing
Bottlebrush explosive red inviting eyes
Honey to lips or bush cordial sweet

> *Honey to lips bottlebrush*
> *Kneeling at altar of God no*
> *Not on this land not here*

Hawes-centricity another world away
Archived Greenough 12 kilometres west
Appetite not here for Hawes' mudpie
Young thirst for knowledge Yamaji

> *Honey to lips bottlebrush*
> *Hawes turned wooden candlesticks*
> *Ghosts sit at Centro Greenough*
> *Not on this land not here*

Sucking nectar bottlebrush sweet
Wattle seeds eating tasting time ago
Visions of firesticks ancestors' walking
Tracks etched into land across land

Honey to lips bottlebrush
Red fire dotted campsites
Culture banished torment real
Wheat grain money worshipped
Not on this land not here

Dance ground feet sand reunite connect
Still wind still ancestors come to visit
Gentle kiss giving to young spirits
Reassuring for the onward journey
Right here on this land right here

Invasion Day
ELIZABETH JARRETT

26th of January
Australia's day to celebrate their nation
Celebrating
Our brave warriors'
Murders and mutilations
Celebrating
Our bravest women's
Rapes and molestations
Celebrating our bond of family
Broken
And torn
By forced separation
All in the name of what?

The great white Australian assimilation

So please explain
Who enjoys a celebration
of the genocide of our first nations? 'It's in the past'
'Get over it,' they say
Okay, so how about we forget about ANZAC Day?

For realise we are still still still
Prisoners of war
Two hundred and twenty-nine years
Of terrorism on our shores
So on today we stand strong together

We have survived
We're black
We're proud
We're strong
And we're alive

Native Tongue
MOJO RUIZ DE LUZURIAGA

I don't speak my Father's native tongue
I was born under a southern sun
I don't know where I belong
I don't know where I belong

My Great-Grandaddy was Wiradjuri
My Father came here from the Philippines
It's where I live, it's where I want to be
Oooh but you make me feel so ill at ease

I don't speak my Father's native tongue
I was born under a southern sun
I don't know where I belong
I don't know where I belong

It's easy enough for you to say
It ain't no thing
But I'm the one you ain't the one
Been living in this skin
So if you want to call me something
Call it to my face
But I will not apologise
For taking up this space
And every time you cut me down
I'm gonna come back fierce
The time is through for being nice
Let's call it what it is

I don't speak my Father's native tongue
I was born under a southern sun
I don't know where I belong
I don't know where I belong

Why Not Be Brothers and Sisters?
STEVEN OLIVER

I'm about to inject some blackness into this here affair
now to be exact
When I say 'black'
It's my Aboriginality I want to declare
See we're 3% of the population
So, to see this shit is rare
Now sit back, relax and embrace what I've got
Cause I've got nothing but love to share …
Okay, I lied
I might share some facts
Facts that pertain to us minority of blacks
Like we're 3% of the population
But we're 27% of the gaols
My own family are statistics when it comes to Aboriginal males
Our life expectancy is shorter by around 10 or so years
That's why in a space of six months, five times I shed tears
See, we're numbing our lives with substance abuse
And if that doesn't work we look for a noose
Our suicide rates among the highest on earth
And people think the answer is to deny us our worth
We should just forget who we are
Act the white way, cause it's the right way
You want a better life?
You better do what the man say
And it just goes around in circles
Over 230 years and we're facing the same hurdles
Asking for the same things we were asking way back when

Like, let us be ourselves on our own lands
This isn't about guilt and it's not about blame
It's not about trying to make people feel shame
Cause see, we'll say it's the white man
Then he says, it's us blacks
And we'll go back and forth till we're talkin' to backs
Or we're sitting in silence, not sayin' a word
Or maybe we're screaming
But not being heard
The truth of it is we're in this together
So why not be brothers and sisters and work for the better?
Why not start talking, lending our ears
Embracing the truth and facing the fears
We all share this land
Every day, every night
So why not look to our plight,
And help make it right?
Cause only when people are truly equal, you see
Is when we can say, we are all free.

Got Ya
KERRY REED-GILBERT

Got ya

I knew he was mine
frothing at the mouth
(literally speaking)
I was waiting for him
my body ready to strike

Like a leopard
on the verge of attack
I waited, biding my time.
I held my breath.

My muscles taut
prepared to pounce
to strike, to maim.

I knew the moment was at hand
the spirits played around him
I watched him fight for courage
to utter the words for me
to slash at his heart
my claws willing to impale him
with a death blow.

Abos – why say sorry to the Abos
we had to teach them to use the knife and fork
they would have been lost without us
Abos – why say sorry to the Abos
I got him, he never knew what hit him,
he will never utter those words again.

Nanna Emily's Poem (Mount Isa Cemetery 2014)
DECLAN FURBER GILLICK

Author's Note

This is a yarn; the words were chosen, structured and sequenced to be spoken by me. It is a piece of oral history. Committing it to paper or even audio recording does the story and its spirit something of a disservice. The yarn came through my body and was originally spoken in my tones and cadences, imbued with the character of my experience. My body is the proper place for it to dwell and to be heard. Those of us committed by choice, duty and love to the oral traditions understand the limitations of the printed word; the immediate compromise of spirit and the potential for erasure and distortion. Whilst I do write for the page, this story, like most of my writing, is for telling. This is my poetic testament, a declaration, my recollection. My evidence. This is our oral history. Nonetheless, within relationships of love and care, where publishers and story-keepers are committed to honouring the delicate nature of story, it is sometimes right to commit our oral history to the page. An oral recording of this piece can be found in volume two of Melbourne Spoken Word's audio magazine, *Audacious*.

Please consider reading this text aloud in a moment of relative stillness or within a small, simple ritual; whatever that might mean to you. This may offer the story's spirit a tone by which to speak more clearly.

Thank you to Alison for taking care of this story. And thank you, reader, for reading my note.

my father was four when he left his mother
my grandmother, Emily Furber
flown across country in a government airplane
clutching at his little sister's hand
looking out the window, down at the red desert
connection to the centre and his mother's breast severed
severed by a government airplane

they were taken to a tiny little island in the tropics
where the sand and the hands that held them there were a
    different colour
to the mother in the sand and the hands that they left
    behind
their border was the water that reminded them that island
    wasn't theirs

thick and heavy, the air in their lungs
the humidity and sweat dampened their neat, crisp clothes

where's mum?
what am I doing here?
what are we doing so far from home?

my father lived on that island for ten years
he learned maths, he learned to read and write
forgot his tribal tongue and forgot his mother's touch
he learned to love the feeling of salt water on his face
he learned to love the feeling of a saddle between his thighs
he learned to find family where there wasn't any

my father and all the other brown-skinned babies
grew up on that island surrounded by water
the sun rose and set
the tide came and went
all his new cousins, they eventually left
off into the world, the great wide world
somewhere on the other side of that endless sea

the mail plane came and went like the tide
and when my father was twelve he got a letter from his sister
to tell him that their mother had died

now fifty-one years later, I'm standing by his side
as he visits nanna's grave for the very first time
he is an ageing man
who has lived a proud life
and been father to many a child
some of them, like me, are his own
others are the children of absent men

now I'm standing barefoot by my grandmother's grave
my voice starts to waver
I look at the tears on my father's face
and I never seen him cry like this

he cradles his akubra
and his head hangs low, pointed down towards the land
and I see for a moment, he allows himself the space
to break open something he's had locked and tucked away
and there, as I'm reading some clumsy words aloud

I look at my father whose head is bowed
and what I see is a boy hold a handwritten letter
that tells him that his mother is dead

his mother who had each of her children stripped from her
shipped into the distance one after the other
and each separated from their sisters and their brother

his mother whose sickness and death were sudden
who was young and black and poor and forgotten
and who's buried where she worked for some whitefella
stockmen
who is buried so far from our home

nah, I never seen him cry like this

on this warm August day in my twenty-fourth year
it is I who must now be a man
to keep my voice steady, I breathe deep and heavy
and I walk over to where he stands
I stand by his side, raise a strong brown arm
over his shoulders as he finally, silently shakes

in the stillness that trails off from my final word
he clears his own throat and he catches his breath

mum, thanks for bringing me into this world
you did
you did
you did your best

Are You Beautiful Today?

ROMAINE MORETON

are you beautiful today?
are your children safe and well,
brother, mother, sister too?
I merely ask so you can tell,

I wish to know your home,
your world,
or any place where you
dwell,
I want to know
are you beautiful,
are you well?

I drag this sorry carcass
have dragged it for centuries,
and miles,
I have dragged it over gnashing teeth,
poised in revolt,
and poised in style,

but I laugh, do you laugh too?
I laugh with my sisters and brothers
at things that others wouldn't get,
while talkin' 'bout jail,
while talkin' 'bout death,

I laugh loud and I laugh hard,
I rumble the mountains from the pit
of my stomach,
while talkin' 'bout jail,
while talkin' 'bout death,

this is a funny situation,
the life of the oppressed,
this is a funny situation,
much funnier than death,

but we cannot be bleak
and we cannot be meek,
we must call upon greatness,
to get us through this week,

and I look for inspiration,
in this misery,
and must say,
I am very inspired,
and it is funny inspiration,
you see,
so funny,
it sometimes grows me
tired,

are you beautiful today,
your brother, mother, sister too?
are you well clothed and well fed,
and are they alive

and
well,
not dead?

can you laugh when trying is
gathered 'round your door,
can you laugh at the crying,
can you laugh and cry for more?

and isn't this inspirational,

I think of the money
I have saved,
'cause I know folk
who take great
treks,
I know folks
who have been
to Tibet,
and I feel so smug
and I feel so small
for what they seek
I find
gathered 'round my door,

and still I laugh,
I laugh and cry
for more,

and isn't this inspiring,

my grandfather,
he wanted to sing,
wanted to bellow
from the trees,
he wanted to sing opera
from the bottom of the river,
he wanted the bees and
their knees,
but he couldn't stop
the laughing
'round his front door,
he couldn't stop his laughing
oh and how it roared,

oh yes he laughed,
he laughed so hard
it killed,
and our family
laughs harder still,
yes our laughter
shakes the hills,
'bout my grandfather,
and his unborn dream,
'bout my grandfather,
and his blissful screams,

are you beautiful,
do you create great things,
do you read beautiful poetry,
and all those other

beautiful things,
I think I would like to too,
you know,
prose, paint and draw,
but I am so addicted to laughing,
it just leaves me wanting more,
like an injection,
like an infection,
and I do not know withdrawal,

I've had to
cross coals and attitudes,
seen my sisters hanging,
and my brothers too,
disease is not far either,
others die from Aids too,

we sit around our lounge rooms,
discussing jail and suicide as though asking
one lump or two?
and all of this makes me laugh,
and I laugh
till I am blue,

I am accosted
by misinformation
when it is said,
ah you are a peaceful people,
your people do love
peace,

oh yes we know beauty,
and yes we know peace,
but peace and beauty
are uninspiring,
unless
you've been
to Greece,

my people shout,
till the highest tree
has heard it,
we brag about poverty,
and say things like,
have you read it,

my people speak loudly,
about those who have fallen before us,
speak proudly,
'bout those who fall
beside
us,

I am not a peaceful person,
simply because I am not
at peace,
if only I could stop laughing,
if only I could
silence
this beast,

are you inspired?

does insecurity
rattle your windows?
and your family
when
they gather,

does insecurity
rattle your perceptions,
and everything
that
matters?

are you beautiful?
and is all well
in your world
today,
are you not condemned
for the things
you might,
or might not
say

are you inspired,
by that which is gathered
'round your door?

does it leave you wanting
does it leave you wanting
for more?

do you find it funny
can you laugh
at the in-betweens,

could you rise each day
to do,
those gotta do
things,

is survival funny,
or has it become
a
chore,

could you laugh
if misery
were crowded
'round your
door?

could you be so inspired,
you would beg and want
for
more,

could you take
your broken heart,
and paint
the most magnificent masterpiece
the world has ever seen,

could you take
the blood of your sister,
and make people
believe
in a
dream,

could you take
conversations about jail and suicide
and make it as though
you were saying
one lump
or
two,

could all of these things
inspire
the brilliance
which you are sure
lives
inside of
you.

Say My Name

MELEIKA GESA-FATAFEHI

Thank you Dad, for my name.
Thank you Mum, for letting me keep it.
Thank you Sydney Nan, for saying my name lovingly every time.
Lastly, thank you Papa and Nan, and the rest of my ancestors,
I dedicate this all to you.

My name was my name before
            I walked among the living
    before I could breathe
    before I had lungs to fill
before my great grandmother passed
       and everyone was left to grieve

My name was birthed from a dream
       a whisper from gods to a king
      a shout into the stars that produced
           another that shone as bright
They held me without being burnt, humming lullabies in pidgin

My name was passed down from my
       ancestors
They acknowledged my roots grew in two
       places
So, they ripped my name from the ocean
       and mixed it into the bloodlines of my totems

My name has survived the destruction of worlds

And the genocidal rebirthing of so-called ones
It's escaped the overwhelmed jaw of the death bringer
        many a time
It has survived the conflicts that resulted in my gods,
        from both lands, knowing me as kin,
But noticing that I am painfully unrecognisable and lost
They are incapable of understanding
        the foreign tongue that was forced on me

My name has escaped cyclones and their daughters
It has been blessed by the dead
As they mixed dirt, salt and liquid red,
        into my flesh
My name is the definition of resilience
It is a warrior that manifested because of warriors

So, excuse me as I roll my eyes or sigh as you
Mispronounce my name
        over and over again
Or when you give me another
        that dishonours my mothers and fathers
That doesn't acknowledge my lineage to my island home
Or the scents of rainforest and ocean foam
You will not stand here on stolen land
        and whitewash my name
For it is two words intertwined
        holding as much power as a hurricane
Say it right or don't say it at all
For I am Meleika
        I will answer when you call

**'Because we want it back,
need it back, because they can'**

– Claire G. Coleman, 'I Am the Road'

Lead You to the Shore

STEVEN OLIVER

After all these years, I am still amazed that I can identify with, as if it's my own story and the stories of those I love, someone else's tales of heartbreak from the other side of the continent. They experience tragedy and frustration in the exact same way my mob and I do. 'I Am the Road' by Claire G. Coleman did such a thing to me, provoked my sense of identity, belonging to my ancestry, my place of birth and where I grew up.

I am descended from the Waanyi, Gangalidda peoples near the Gulf of Carpentaria, the Kuku Yalanji people of the Daintree, the Woppaburra mob of Great Keppel Island and of the Bundjalung and Biripi nations in New South Wales. I was born on Mitakoodi country, known as Cloncurry north-west Queensland, and grew up on Wulgurukaba and Bindal lands, known as Townsville. I had to make peace with the label forced upon my ancestors, the label of Aboriginal. Identity and sense of self meant aligning my being with a name pushed upon the Old People. There were no Aboriginal people here over two hundred years ago. There were no blacks, blackfellas, Aborigines, Aboriginals, First Nations, natives, Indigenous, First Australians, Original Australians, Traditional Owners, First People, original occupants or – the favourites of racists – 'abos', 'boongs' or 'coons'. There was the Waanyi, Gangalidda, Woppaburra, Bundjalung, Biripi, Kuku Yalanji, Mitakoodi, Wulgurukaba, Bindal and hundreds of other clans, peoples, countries.

And here I am, this kid from Cloncurry who grew up in Townsville. Who travelled the eight hundred kilometres to and from each place either by train or by road more times than I could ever try to guess (and who now flies everywhere) and who, in this moment, finds himself once more a child, sitting in a car with a towel stuck in the window to block the sun and its accompanying heat and, in turn, leads me to ask: who was that child and is he who he wanted to be, apart from Superman?

I've read through 'Chocolate Wrappers' by Pauline Whyman twice and, although I'm feeling the urge to read it multiple times to fully grasp it, I've decided not to for now. Is the intent to fill you with so much rich language that you inflate your blood sugar? That reading it can be too much and instead of overwhelming your body with sugar, it expertly overwhelms your mind with language.

When people say English is a tricky language, I say: 'That's because it's used to trick people'; gives them a false sense of security to manipulate them into another's bidding.

For quite a while now I've often seen the irony (and sadness) in having to use the English language to convey messages about what is killing Aboriginal people, when the use of English is killing our languages. People in this country argue over the bogus notion that their 'free speech' is being taken from them yet don't even realise that, in depending on being told everything by government and media, they've given up their free thought. Words can be beautifully descriptive or beautifully deceptive depending on who's writing and who's reading, who's seeing or not seeing. People think they know what they've read but have no idea what it said.

'Move on Black' by Jim Everett is so loaded I would need much more than a few hundred words to deconstruct it. It parodies how we are always asked to let go of our history and traditions. But for us, traditions are not history, even history isn't really history. They are constant and alive. History informs the now and to look at time as a separate entity by breaking it into parts as if it can be separated into a point of fact does an injustice to time. What is modern, and who decides in a cyclical world? Time is a powerful thing that binds us all.

We're at a place where we don't know ourselves anymore. People must question their connectedness to all that was, all that is and all that is going to be. To stop looking and start feeling, remembering what it means to be part of something greater. This can't go on, this fraying. This constant separation. This unwillingness to acknowledge another. Our isolation is destroying where we are, where we are to go and obliterates where we have come from. We're running forward so fast that when we need to find our way back to our beginning, we won't know from where we came, from darkness.[1]

I read 'Old Clever Woman' by Ken Canning/Burraga Gutya after reading 'Move on Black', which made it all the more powerful. Especially when you consider the last line of each poem.

We transition from:

You can do it, move on Black

to

She wait all same – never go, / she keepin' pink demon movin' on.

This in turn made me look at the notion of 'move' or 'moving' and the way we use it in a physical or metaphorical sense. That thought takes me to my favourite line from the song 'My Mind' by Yebba, who sings: 'I sure won't stay, but I'll be damned if I ever leave.' Whether or not she chooses to physically stay with the cheating partner but lets her mind leave this place of torment, or whether she chooses to leave him but can't move past the cheating, is both powerful and heartbreaking at the same time.

When non-Indigenous people ask us to move on, they assume that we want to be stuck in a painful place. That we love having to constantly get angry, annoyed, upset, political or any of the other words they love applying to us when standing up for ourselves. You can dress me up, have me speak English, work with you in your way of working and I'll move that way, but my connection to, and value in, being Aboriginal will never be moved. Whenever people ask me, 'Why do you Aboriginal people have to be different? Why can't you just be like us?', I reply, 'We don't have to be different, we just are different. The real question is, why do you need us to be like you?'

In a world that has come to consider making money all sacred and powerful, I loved the excerpt from Kevin Buzzacott's 'Lake Eyre Is Calling, Ankaku for Life'. Our obligation and responsibility to each other as part of humanity far outweighs our own bewildering desire to ooh and ah at pretty lights and sparkly stones that you can't eat, drink or breathe. Are we that depressed at our state of the world that we need to distract ourselves with anything to make us happy?

I read through 'Custodial Seeds' by Yvette Holt enough times to feel as if I shouldn't be reading it at all. Like I'm intruding and being voyeuristic. Yvette's language is beautiful, as always, and also, as always, strong. I can't help but feel that this is for the eyes of women only. That being male, I'm an outsider overstepping boundaries when I follow the subject along the river. I follow to learn, but it is not my knowledge to know.

'Visiting' by Tony Birch spoke to me of loss and longing. An aching yearning for what once was but is simply now a sad memory. I felt no joy yet it felt like there should have been. Like it should've been joyous in remembering youth but instead it's a sadness that youth is lost. That in his youth lay the one person who understood the narrator but, instead of being by their side, they have been lost to time either through paths going in different directions or life for one has ended and therefore so does another's. That instead of a cleansing, the water sinks into the soul to soak it with a sadness that stains the heart of the sole speaker. Who takes it all in – the water, the memories, the emotion, the longing, the hurt – as if they were a sponge now made heavy by it all. It's almost as though the water isn't birthing life but drowning what remains. It felt heavy to me, yet not as a downpour or flooding, but as a current that takes you and one that you can't fight but simply have to go along with and you can only hope it'll lead you to the shore.

I liked 'Cult-charr Jammer' by Paul Collis. I think everyone has culture, or at least everyone has 'a' culture. We need clarity on what exactly we mean when we say culture. For me, I've been fortunate enough to grow up learning songs and dances, and they've been things that have helped cement my identity and speak strongly of culture. Which culture, though? North Queensland culture, blackfella culture, Aboriginal culture, language groups culture, Indigenous culture, and First Nations culture. Perhaps it's now even an amalgamation of cultures that has been the product of the dominating culture that is one of appropriating and assimilating and what we have left for some of us is now 'our' culture. Remnants that may seem to be fragile or incomplete but still strong enough to solidify who we are by way of being not what others try to make us into but being connected to the myriad of cultures that existed upon this land for thousands of years.

I shouldn't really speak too far on this as I am not an authority on culture so not deemed fit to speak of it. What I will say is I think we all should learn, where we can, the songs and dances of our mobs, and we should use them as a display of identity, sovereignty, resistance, pride, affirmation and honouring. How can some of us say we're proud Aboriginal people but be embarrassed to sing our songs and perform our dances?

This word Jukurrpa (or Tjukurpa) has been finding its way to me a lot. From Zaachariaha Fielding from Electric Fields who told me of my personal Tjukurpa, from the Art Gallery of NSW where I encountered art related to Tjukurpa, from my artist mate Mark Horton who I first met last year when he painted me for the Archibald and now from Pansy Rose Napaljarri in 'The Changing Face of the Jukurrpa'.

People might think that I move in circles where I would hear that word often. I've worked in this business for thirty years and only recently has it been constant. I've been on this journey now where I feel I'm being led. There's something greater going on here. It's daunting trying to interpret and articulate it. I only know it's important we take heed and start hearing and seeing and feeling it. There are so many things in this poem that I can connect to my life to show something bigger than me is happening, but I will give you one example. Pansy Rose Napaljarri writes: *From dark corners / of the hidden caves / into galleries / hung / dot dot painting / people see and wonder, / 'What does it mean?'*

Whenever Aboriginal people do something, such as make a piece of art or sing a song or perform a dance, it's viewed in a critical way to deconstruct it. It's compared to Van Gogh, Pavarotti or a work of ballet, and is often seen as simplistic or spiritual, with the word 'spiritual' transformed into multiple meanings that people are interpreting in a multitude of ways. The extremities of the 'spiritual' range from being called mythological, mystical, outright bullshit to enlightening, awakening, transformative, rebirth. People look at our art –

whether visual or performative art – and try to see what it's trying to say with the selfish act of what does it mean to them, when they should be trying to hear what it says and ask: what do they, Aboriginal people, mean to our humanity? What is the truth of our connection to one another told through the offering of art?

Sometimes you can't see the world; sometimes you have to hear it and other times require you to feel it. That is how you fully learn who you are and only then you finally understand who we, as as a people, are. Seeing only gives one part of a truth that you can bend to suit selfish needs. Hearing and feeling give you the whole picture, what some may call truth.

We are trying – and have been trying for hundreds of years – to show you who we are, but all you do is see who we are not: you. We're not telling you to only see us – we're only saying to see you within us. That's connectedness. When we understand our connection to each other, the land and all that exists upon it, then we understand our place in all things and our belonging. That's when we understand what it 'spiritually' means to be us.

---

[1] A quote from an earlier draft of my play *From Darkness*.

I Am the Road

CLAIRE G. COLEMAN

My grandfather was the bush, the coast, salmon gums,
   hakeas, blue-grey banskias
Wind-whipped water, tea-black estuaries, sun on grey stone
My grandfather was born on Country, was buried on Country
His bones are Country
I am the road

I was born off Country, in that city
I hear, less than two-weeks old I travelled Country
A bassinet on the back seat of the Kingswood
I remember travels more than I remember a home
I am the road

My father is the beach, the peppermint tree, the city back
   when, before it was a city
My father is the ancient tall-tree Country, between his father
   Country and that town
My father is World War II, his father was a soldier
My father wandered, worked on rail, drove trucks
I am the road

Campgrounds up and down that coast were the childhood
   home of my heart
Where my memories fled, where my happiness lived
Campgrounds in somebody else's stolen Country
I am the road

The road unrolls before me
My rusty old troopy wipes oily sweat from its underside on
    the asphalt
Says, 'I am here, I am here'
The engine breathes in, breathes out, pants faster than I can
Sings a wailing thundering song
Wraps its steel self around me and keeps me safe,
    a too large overcoat
I am the road

I slept, for a time, on the streets of Melbourne
No Country, no home, as faceless as the pavement
I was dirt on the streets, as grey as the stone, as the concrete
I am the road

We showed explorers where the water was
They lay their road over our path, from water to water
Lay a highway over their road, tamed my Country with their
    highway
I am the road

My Boodja has been stolen, raped, they dug it up,
    took some of it away
They killed our boorn, killed our yonga, our waitch, damar, kwoka
Put in wheat and sheep, no country for sheep my Boodja
My Country, most of it is empty, the whitefellas have no use
    for it
Except to keep it from us
Because we want it back, need it back, because they can
I am the road

People ask where I am from, I cannot simply answer
To mob, I am Noongar, South Coast. I am Banksias,
    wind on waves on stone
To travellers, whitefella nomads, I am from where I live –
    that caravan over there
To whitefellas from Melbourne who see how I drink my coffee
I must be from Melbourne, I am not Melbourne
I am the road

One day wish to, hope to, dream, buy some of my
    grandfather's Country back
Pay the thieves for stolen goods
Theft is a crime, receiving stolen goods is a crime
Until one day
I am the road

Old Clever Woman

KEN CANNING/BURRAGA GUTYA

Old woman sitting by the road
waiting long time this one.
Tree keep hot sun out,
thinkin' hummin' old songs.
Leave hand mark in dust,
for big one wind take away
to her place of secret
she knows but not tellin'.
Slow dronin' noise comin'
along a road like one big firefly.
This be that fella bus
fulla starin' one – pink face.
They lot silly that one
sittin' long – long time
on motor – hardly touchin' earth.
Close now drone roars,
demons from night time.
Big squeal – call him break,
alla time hurtin' ears.
Eyes shades over push em away,
alla same captain cook.
They makin' funny noise,
not talkin' – sorta like wild chook,
click – click – click – click,
they just love picture,
no remember – head must be empty.
click – click – click – click,

the guns shoot fire,
little ones screaming,
scream never go away.
Pink faces make same no talk noises.
This old one got one big photo,
killin' times her mob dyin'
click – click alla same.
This lot take picture
put 'em in big book.
Tell 'em world they good,
they just love blackfella.
Click – click – same one,
gun – camera no matter,
all part of killin' thing.
So she sits all day
she's there all time,
waiting for big one firefly,
carryin' wongi pink people.
She bin worryin' – greivin'.
Pink mob need photos,
makin' they feel good fella.
No picture – they go lookin'
maybe find big mob,
plenty trouble that one.
No more picture then,
they want alla people,
alla land – they take away.
Bring grog make wongi dance,
she bin waitin' before road,
just dirt track for horse.

Bus – horse same bad things.
She wait all same – never go,
she keepin' pink demon movin' on.

The Changing Face of the Jukurrpa
PANSY ROSE NAPALJARRI

Under the shade of the mulga tree
two wrinkle faced
old yapa men
sit
yarning 'bout their
good ol' days
when life was what
it really was meant to be.

Ceremonies
all night long
under the thousand stars
gleaming bright light of the moon
reflections on the waterhole
nearby
sending rays of light.

Happy painted faces
yapa kids
ready to dance
clapsticks clapsticks
beating the rhythm of the age-old
music.

Excited
as laughter fills the air
dancers

here and there
everywhere
painted up
with the rich colours
of the Earth
ready to perform
the ancient dances of the
Dreamtime
The Jukurrpa comes alive.

Beautiful songs of the Dreamtime
since beginning of time
journey of my people
into the Milky Way.
Red dust stamping
black feet
stamping
buried in the sand dancing
to the rhythm of the clapsticks.

Secret language
spoken by all
understood by all
darkness covers the sky
time to begin
the ancient ceremonies of the
Jukurrpa.

Jukurrpa still here
seen differently

through many eyes
the world watching.

From dark corners
of the hidden caves
into galleries
hung
dot dot painting
people see and wonder,
'What does it mean?'

Ceremonies
performed
red nagas
white headbands
microphone
cameras flashing
more more.

Misplaced droning sound
fills the air
airconditioned room
sea of faces
hearing
the haunted sound of
The Dreamtime.

New technology
crept in
from the dark

like a black spirit
from amongst the mist
of the unknown world.

Into the Jukurrpa
bringing new changes
for the better or worse
nobody knows yet.

Shining black jets
state of art
zooming
across the sky
destination unknown.

Seeds of destruction
sown of Mother Earth.

Alcohol
killing our people
once proud
now down.

Changing world
goes hand-in-hand
with the Dreamtime
new technology
old Jukurrpa.

Cult-charr Jammer
PAUL COLLIS

Yo!

Whitefullas got no cult-charr!
– Only me
With my arm fulla tatts, up my sleeve.

– Only Us Mob!
Only *us*
Got cult-charr.

Don't tell me! I lived it, man. Us bruvas, we live it –
Everyday man. We fuken live it.
Blak and Proud. Deadly, un'a?

Always was
Always will be
ABORIGINAL LAND.

Colonisation is *YOURS* whitefulla.

Blak, proud and deadly …
King Billy,
Queenie,
Grandfather,
Grandmother,
Emu in the sky

– they're MINE, whitefulla!! NOT YOURS!
What you got, whitefulla?
You git lost. You steal. You kill my country.

You poisoned us.
Kill our water.
Try to wipe us mob out, whitefulla.

Emu in the sky watchin' all this –
Murrdie kids on the ground, watchin' all this too.
Always was – always will be –

ABORIGINAL LAND!

Red, Black, Yellow.
Only I can know *this* country!

'Un'a?'

Move on Black

JIM EVERETT

You are not young, don't look back
Only two hundred years this game has run
First they come to seize your land
Bringing poison and rule of gun
The moves you've made have been controlled
Because traditions you would not break
Home the Dreamtime could ever hold
The reality for your children's sake

On through time you have held back
Not letting go of any past
While your children move in a modern world
Traditionalism holds you fast
The token face you give the whites
Because they control you to behave
Is the very thing that nulls your might
As token blacks they'll keep you safe

The way I see has many heads
And things to do to blend your future
Keeping all the people's knowledge
With changes coming ever faster
Stand competing with modern minds
Not using a past they cannot see
Your history but a point of fact
By itself a weakening plea

Your nation can survive the change
As tribal ways become the weaker
To beat the white man's power binge
Their way forces the only future
So keep your people's heritage strong
By staying on the modern track
I see your victories coming on
You can do it, move on Black.

Chocolate Wrappers
PAULINE WHYMAN

I slept with chocolate wrappers
Not the rappers with chocolate skin
The Lindt chocolate kind

Upon waking
Head winds blow outside
Accountable story telling fragments
In night skies illuminated
Predominately scarred burrows of time withered
Beneath an abhorrent tide of catastrophy
Echoing songs and sins creeping
Morosely below my shining
Black eyes of mud sticking to weeds
Of sorrow drowned twice before now
Awoken living on jagged oyster beds
Shredding fellow soles
Accompanied by melancholy
And bound by mournful echoes of colonial violence
With deepened renewal of sovereign unity
We gather a feathered bed of nurture
And reach out to bamboozled heads
Shrieking on those winds
Passing over lonely barren
Hilltops once stood dappling
Effects from lush trees and shrubs
Alive and moving constantly
Yet still!

Calm
Breathing
Consciously diving into thoughts and feelings
And hearts lampooned sideways
Through unexpected voices
Ranging intonations and intentions
Shatter barbarous fence lines and minds introduced
Introduced DNA in your marrow of your bones
Connected to daydreaming hollows of gaunt faces
Wrenching clammy hands reach for you and you wake
With a sudden fright of your own despair. SUGAR!
Sugar is a killer of my people drenching
Its sweet sticky joyous tender kisses on your lips
Anticipating a magnificent journey into suspended animation
As to the lure of centuries past practices
Enslaving your body and mind incapacitating love
Opponents of you scour the edges of every continent;
any land they see
Whereby they have sweetened the hardened sea water on
the trade winds
    And ocean flows
Their notorious DESTRUCTION FLOWS in your veins
A lesson of denial approaches head on and smashes
Tiny innocent minds and bodies and emaciates the
human structure
Of life
SUGAR!
Sugar is a killer of my people

Custodial Seeds

YVETTE HOLT

And so she followed the river
doing as she was told
a long wide shimmering snake
sparkling across the moonlit current
dividing neighbours between
economics and class.

Walking until she could walk no further
collapsing beside a retired rivergum tree
she leans against its weathered body
stretching limbs from a pillar of nature
resisting the push for life
tasting the sap from a torso of knowledge.

Lifting up her homemade dress
she squats above the earth
warm odourless liquid rushes between her
legs, cleansing the dirt
enriching the soil with a river of yolk.

Finally her night cries deliver
resonating tears before a disturbing sunrise
the rope of life now rests on her flowing breasts
and again the canine bastards cross the river
digging a bowl for their midnight desire.

Visiting
TONY BIRCH

For Stephen

I trace your life at points along the river; below the Cat-Walk where we hung like sleeping bats from the rusting girders we left behind to fall through heat for the touch of silken waters waiting to meet us sixty feet below. We lifted the skirts of Skipping Girl, strobing the night with her erratic neon rhythm. Her beauty lit a riverbank infested with years of stolen car wrecks and trapped wet lovers. Until the day they dressed her and ordered the girl to dance for the peak-hour crawl, homeward bound to the emptiness of suburban life. The river's edge is beautified now, the bridges are caged in safety, Deep Rock lies drowned beneath a strip of freeway and the long-abandoned sweat shops dazzle with the glass and steel of the market. Sitting at the falls again, I skip stones and think of us, together here on summer nights. We carried this river home with us, her love entangled in rich hair and staining our young skin.

Lake Eyre Is Calling: Ankaku for Life
KEVIN BUZZACOTT

We've got the experts;
    we've got the professors,
        we've got the scientists.
We've got our mob. They know everything.
Nobody can look after the country better than us.
Them fellas can't look after the country; land care, whatever.

They don't know this country.
    – too old!
        – too big!
            – come from too far!

So their legislations and policies and that,
I don't trust anything mob.
Nothing.

These are the only things I know; these sticks,
and Old People, and the country.
Here in the heart, hold 'em in the heart –
that's the only thing I know that can take me home.

Behind Enemy Lines
PROVOCALZ AND ANCESTRESS

Kept in solitary confinement for twenty-three-and-a-half hours a day, for fifteen days straight, he's lost all sense of time and he's deeply distressed. The boy's been asking the guards repeatedly for weeks why he's being kept in solitary confinement and when he's going to be released from his dark, hot, stinking cell.

Provocalz
Fuck a Royal Commission, brah
These royals' commission
The invasion, the genocide, the conditions
Where we're prisoners of war
The system at its core
Is a child on the floor getting kicked in the jaw
Stripped of culture, saw that black cockatoo
Flying over the yard, that's freedom he never knew
Buried in them walls with sadistic screws
Who couldn't give two fucks, so they torture and abuse
Rehabilitation of a future that's sacred
Never happens in the lockup, brah, that shit breeds hatred
Gotta fight to survive, that could have been me
Young cunt doing crime, life on these streets
Just a product of them hard times, honest
We tried, did our parents even want us?
Empty pockets, so I'm out to make a profit
Carry tools for protection and ain't talking about a socket

The most innocent of lives in a cold, dark cell
They're forgotten, like they're in another realm
Getting welcomed into hell by a devil in a uniform
Failed life so he's out to fucking ruin yours
What's the cause and effect? There's no rest for us all
War of attrition, only listen when we're forced
Bound and gagged, so you know it's fuck them all
Thrown in the paddy by your pigger over laws
That were built on bloodshed, the death congregation
Of this ugly nation
Another black death and the government are racists
All we've got is us feeling trapped and invaded
Deep in them cages and ain't even got a plan
Right here on my land as I raise my hand
Bedsheet gripped tight round my neck as I cry
Because ending my own life's the only way I will survive

The image you've just seen isn't from Guantanamo Bay or Abu Ghraib, but Australia in 2015. A boy, hooded, shackled, strapped to a chair and left alone. It is barbaric: a system that punishes troubled children instead of rehabilitating them.

Ancestress

Murder, neglect and disrespect
Is all we can expect from an illegitimate government
The colonial context will never relent
Till we get our land back again
Maybe then we can be friends
When the pain begins to mend
Till then, keep your hands off our children

Hey Mr PM,
We all know you turned your back when you first seen them
But still you pretend
Dance around your lies and your policies
In our babies' eyes
Spirits dance around campfires, corroborees
Don't you see, this is still daylight robbery
Nobody's free
Everything the government has done to us is shady
Always been torturing our babies
Swear ya tryna send us crazy
The oppression's filling spaces trans-generationally
Through our ancestry
And it's never gonna stop it seems
I guess u can't even have proppa dreams
A world without a child's screams
Without the violence and torture
For your sons and daughters
Maybe there's something in the water
I think it's all the bloodshed and slaughter
That your people taught ya

But hey maybe it's time to just reflect on the concept
And stop all the nonsense
Be honest about your hand in the torment
Unlock the cage, because nothing's going to change
Till we get our land back again
Maybe then we can be friends
When the pain begins to mend
Till then, be a better man
And keep your hands off our children

'This I would tell you'

– Oodgeroo Noonuccal, 'Son of Mine'

Medicine In, Obligation Out

ALI COBBY ECKERMANN

It is an honour to respond to this selection of poems. The challenge was how best to highlight the implication contained in each work, so superseded by style. There was little I could say; the poems stood on their own merit. I felt each poem reiterated the telling of stories, linked by the intergenerational experiences that often repeat without repair. I wanted to highlight how our history repeats. Every poem exists as part of that cycle. The poems show how the Western models of poetry and linear time are charades in Aboriginal poetry. For me, it was important to rejoice at how the weaving of language is resurgent. I felt excited as during this process the poets' names created their own signature poem of lives, experiences and families.

It was impossible to move from the emotive impact of the two poems written to Denis Walker. The first poem, 'Son of Mine', was written by his mother Oodgeroo Noonuccal in 1986. Completing the cycle is the poem 'Grandfather of Mine', written by his granddaughter Elizabeth Walker in 2018. How can I add reverence to that which is so revering?

Denis Walker, who passed into spirit in 2017, remains one of Aboriginal Australia's leading activists, endlessly fighting for our sovereign rights on our unceded land. In doing so, he paved the furrows with seeds of decolonising and truth. We can feel the harvest in the heart of these evolving poets.

As the product of this and other harvests, poetry has become a medicine. I believe there's always a cathartic element of writing, especially in those early years when we do it for the first time and stumble and stagger and leap into our truth. And there's definitely a freedom in finally finding the confidence to articulate a lifetime of feeling and a lifetime that has often felt ill with rejection. In that freedom comes a righting of the wrongs. These are such poems that give us as their writers and readers a medicine for these wrongs if we choose to take it.

Poetry – including these poems – is also a little bit like a seesaw. You're never tipped over on one side, but the heaviness moves you back and forth. Medicine in. But then in my experience it does tend to tilt the other way I think with the responsibility. Obligation out. Back and forth. Medicine in and obligation out. In my life, as those old Ngangkaris and Law people who taught me the value of living a cultured life passed away, I felt a huge responsibility to honour them. I had to respect those years filled with so much love.

Some of the best poems that I've ever heard were shared around a campfire at the Aboriginal Writers Retreat, a small venture I created in 2009 at my home on Ngadjuri land, in Koolunga. Their writers then chucked them into the flames. People said they didn't want them published. Other Stolen Generations people were sharing their pain on the page and then burning it. And that was it. Honouring what is only said to a smaller audience. Honouring that these poets may have done, said and burned even more powerful things than what appear in this collection. The campfire is a vessel that holds many of our stories.

As a writer and publisher I felt like, 'Oh my god, I so wanted to publish that poem, that should be shared with the world, it was so beautiful.' But I learned to honour the listener within me. The best reward was in the morning, just seeing something shift in their eyes or, you know, there was something different. Often the poem is more than what gets published. In our cycles of poetry we have to remember that there is more out there, in the embers of a fire somewhere. It had to be spoken, and now it has been. It is remembered in a different way.

I have a bit of melancholy every now and again for those years I spent in the desert. That's necessary some days, but not necessary for too long. My lifespan is getting shorter. None of us knows what the future holds. These poems remind us of that urgency. Personally I think there's a little bit more that those Old People want me to say, and I'm listening and learning to articulate it in a more precise way. So we've got to honour that and get busy writing and then get our words published into the mainstream, because, sadly, twelve years of the intervention, and a hundred years ... one hundred and fifty years ... two hundred years of the Stolen Generations, our children are still being removed, the deaths in custody continue as incarceration rates climb.

None of the issues that have been written about and are of constant concern to Aboriginal people and our families has shifted. We have to keep writing poetry as a testament to this concern. Medicine in and obligation out.

There's an element of our writing now as Aboriginal people that's writing to the future. Young people are going to discover our poetry in the archives, along with the other Aboriginal brothers and sisters from around the world who are writing and winning awards. And you know: we're quite a force. This selection of poetry certainly shows us that. We're writing the truth on our pages, almost like cement. Our poetry is now permanent. Even if we never see the changes in our lifetime, it's there for another generation in the future.

Part of the reason I say writing for the future is because a lot of archives that have been hidden from Aboriginal eyes are now floating up towards the surface. So, I'm thinking that our poetry, novels, scripts and essays will also bubble up when required. Aboriginal literature will prove to be an archive of truth that we create. Our words will stand against the government policies that were written to govern us.

As we honour the past, honour this terrible past, we are also writing about our fantastic resilience. There it is still. Our hope comes from the Aboriginal community. It's the funny things, the funny moments, the things that define us. Our resilience; our cleverness. We're always bloody diminished for our cleverness. We're seen as people who need the help of others, or are second-class citizens, or less intelligent. I really have a responsibility to write against that warped view of us.

I used to think the creative process happened in my alone time, sitting on my milk crate looking at the sky pretending the Old People were there. I'm not so sure now. It's important to spend time in community too; it's important to travel. That's going to be the impetus of my writing in the next short future; it's how we continue to learn. Cultural education is ongoing – it is a duty of a lifetime. And if you can't express yourself and your truth and you can't honour your story, if no-one is honouring your story, then it's the mental illness, it's the anger, it's those other behaviours that we see and are judged by because, again, people don't take the time to understand the origin. These poems are taking the time. They are honouring the story.

Sadly, I think that a lot of people who come to listen only listen and don't respond. When you've read these poems, also act. As a collective we need to shift the responses because, as Aboriginal people, we are breaking our backs and giving everything of ourselves in the hope for change, and it's not coming.

Bleep bleep! I can't say what I want to really say, I'm bleeping myself, I'm censoring myself, because as a grandmother I'm getting tired. The most rewarding tonic for me is listening to the younger poets, and there are many featured here. What beautiful warriors of resistance and truth. Because we have always been, and always will be.

Much of this essay is a transcription of Ali Cobby Eckermann's conversation with Astrid Edwards on The Garret podcast, 29 August 2019, thegarretpodcast.com/ali-cobby-eckermann

Son of Mine

OODGEROO NOONUCCAL

To Denis

My son, your troubled eyes search mine,
Puzzled and hurt by colour line.
Your black skin soft as velvet shine;
What can I tell you, son of mine?

I could tell you of heartbreak, hatred blind,
I could tell of crimes that shame mankind,
Of brutal wrong and deeds malign,
Of rape and murder, son of mine;

But I'll tell instead of brave and fine
When lives of black and white entwine,
And men in brotherhood combine –
This would I tell you, son of mine.

Grandfather of Mine

ELIZABETH WALKER

For Papa Denis

Papa your weary eyes meet mine,
Worn and tired of hatred blind,
Exhausted from fighting for so much time,
What can I tell you, Grandfather of mine?

You endured crimes that shame mankind,
Survived brutal wrongs and deeds malign,
So let's not speak of sorrow, and repine,
Let's talk of something else, Grandfather of Mine?

Let's talk of triumphs along the line,
Of unwavering efforts that never resign,
Of how you empowered our people with your heart aligned,
Of the difference you made, Grandfather of mine.

Let's talk again of brave and fine,
Of how your struggles lessened mine,
Of how I walk, and dance, shine,
Because of you, Grandfather of mine.

I Run ...
MELANIE MUNUNGGURR-WILLIAMS

I like to call myself a runner
Cos that's what I do
When life attacks me from all angles like I'm a paper bag in
a thunderstorm
I run

I run from all my problems, tune out all sounds of day and
life
Until the only sound I'm left with is my feet hitting the
tarmac, carrying me away, my heart thumping deep
within the lonely, hollow, cavity of my chest
I run

I do fun runs and marathons to escape cyclonic turmoil, run
through rivers in the hope my scent will get lost in the
currents
But like a black tracker, my problems find me
They chase me down the way white authorities chased down
brown-skin babies, hold me captive the way this country
holds asylum seekers and taunt me the way my abuser
does, despite me already leaving the scene of that crime
I run

I run through beautiful boundaries that segregate real from
true,
Run into a blur of horizons of sadness and the gravitational
pull of a woman going mad

Nice girl to bitch, good guy to arsehole, the cycle posing the
   same question as, 'What came first?
The chicken or the egg?'
And the answer ... no one really knows
But personal perspective tells me the nice girl came before
   the arsehole who created the bitch and now I'm stuck
   with trying to run from her, that beat-down beauty,
   suicidal psycho caught between the western white-man's
   world and ancient Aboriginal antiquity
I run

I run to the hills and sing my praises to my inner child cos
   she reminds me of the beauty of a rainbow in the rain,
The excitement of mud between my toes, the happiness of
   life's simplicities, she is the first pearl in my ocean
I run to the ocean where all my tears from years past have
   collected, knowing that if I blow it a kiss the least it will
   do is wave back,
And if I'm lucky
My salty sweat from all that I have run from
Will one day
Bathe me clean

My Ancestors

SACHEM PARKIN-OWENS

Each word I speak, every poem that speaks to you.
The dampened cries of My Ancestors are heard too.
Sky blue truths.
They speak not of life and death,
Rather of hope and survival.

Ginda giba nariyuba (You are my young man)

My Ancestors' skin left wounded and filled with their ochre
    stories.
These wounded stories brimmed my budding stainless mind.
So much so they have grown to be my Child's lullaby.
Just to keep them alive.

Ngari Dege (I am your Ancestor)

My Ancestors' words fall upon me like dusk upon dawn;
Sovereignty and Freedom.
With closed eyes
I search for the origin of my hidden soul through each line;
And through each line
I rewrite and retell
I realise, each rhyme, every poem I write, isn't mine.
They belong to the sovereign and free.
My Ancestors.

Ginda giba nariyuba (You are my young man)
Giba Jagi binji (With fire in your belly)
Bujirang Jabur (Don't be frightened boy)
Ngari Dege (I am your Ancestor)
Wagari Ngali (Carry me) Gana ngayi (Hear me)
Gana nariba jagi (Hear my tribal spirit)
Yara Yari ngiyariya bunji (Go tell your Brothers)
Yara Yari ngiyariya jadin (Go tell your sisters)
(Through your art)
Nyinda yara ba (you go then)

So here I am
A mere man
With a piece of paper and a pen in either hand,
Hands together, not to pray but to put ink to paper,
Retelling 229 more years of lullabies

Gana ngayi (Hear me)

I write from the heart
The source of my ink
Each line I write
Isn't written from what I think
Rather what is held close to my heart;
My Ancestors.

Ngari gana nginda (I hear you)

Justice for Youth
DYLAN VOLLER

When I close my eyes I feel the hits to my head. But don't
get me started on all the abuse and torment.
I was only eleven years I didn't know If It was Right or
Wrong. But what I know now is theese Assaults went on
for way to Long.
Sitting in that chair with a hood over my head. For the whole
two and a half hours I was Just wishing I was Dead.
I remember that time [name removed] told me to kill myself.
I thought about it for days If only you could feel the pain
I felt.
I'm not gonna lie theres been times I have cried. And
thought to myself am I gonna die in side.
I have a lot of questions I really want answered. Like why
wern't my first cry's out for help ever answered.
Does [name removed] Really not care. Or is [they] telling the
truth and [they] didn't know what was going on in there.
Why can't [name removed] Admit [they] was wrong. Instead
of pointing fingers and passing the Blame Along.

I would like to dedicate this poem to [censored] all the other Juveniles that were
subject to this sort of treatment. And if the People who did this to me see's this
I want you to know that I will never be able to forget it happened because it is
stuck in my head. But I have found room in my heart to forgive you as I have
also made mistakes and I hope one day I can also be forgiven for my mistakes.
Thank you
Dylan James Dudley Voller

Remember
LANIYUK

To my wetji Muradoop Kathleen McGinnes Mills
and all Indigenous Matriarchs everywhere

Barangaroo of the Eora was the essence of Resistance
Second wife to Bennelong she bore more than children
She was proud, headstrong, calculated and persistent
She did not fall for the illusion of white ascendance
She defied it
Fought it
Cut throat tore at it
Conspired with the ancestors and reminded the children
Beware the sweet poison in white man's hand
Remember your people, take care of your land
She ripped and tugged at European dresses
Refused red wine and demanded resistance

Truganini of the Palawa possessed the
intelligence of subtle Defiance
Having witnessed the ways of white man's violence
Death, destruction and disease
Lynching, raping, murdering
She knew the tactics of war are not always with spears
And attempted to compromise to the colonial ears
Her negotiations were met with lies and deceit
Her people were dying by foreign disease
She took to the bush with a gun in hand and became
    an outlaw to the white man

Carried her spirit to the Kulin Nations and fought for her
    people's emancipation

My great Kungarakan wetji, Alyandabu, embodied Resilience
A paperbark woman
Lean and pensive
Her family and tribe were killed by rat poison
When her husband died, the state took her children
She worked for white families and when the chores were done
She walked to the township with scraps for her sons
I see her hands holding theirs over walls and through fences
Telling them stories of our people's creation
Now there's apartments from ocean to high ground
Attempting to disguise the Kahlin compound

When the colony decides the story is his
The contributions of our women
Become whitewashed myths

I imagine the nights our women lay awake
Searching the stars, now I do the same
When I watch the skies, I'm holding their gaze
When I breathe in the gum, I carry their names
I can hear them singing on the arrival of rain
Their strength emblazoned in my DNA

Wirritjiribin
KIRLI SAUNDERS

*Wirritjiribin (the lyrebird) is the most knowledgeable creature on
Gundungurra Country. In the Dreaming Story of the waratah,
Wirritjiribin is the one who remembers. The lyrebird is one
of Kirli's personal totems.*

Arise wirritjiribin
tangara your truth
across the daoure
mirren ngununggula yoongaba
to the winyooa

Lyrebird — the one who Remembers

Arise lyrebird
dance your truth
across the earth
sing sings of the people
to the sun

Written on Gundungurra Country with Gundungurra translations informed
by Aunty Velma Mulcahy and Aunty Trish Levett

Haunted House
RAELEE LANCASTER

i.
when my cousin told me her house was haunted
                         i replied: of course it is

how can it not be

when they built buildings on the bones of the broken
used our skeletons to frame the walls of her lego house

she told me to get over it
chose to ignore the screams
         the taste of blood
         the smell of rot

ii.
my cousin told me her house was haunted
by a little old english lady with purple hair and no children

it couldn't be anyone else her
psychic friend told her so

i reminded her that our great-grandfather was shot dead
just down the road; and how the elders said there was a massacre site
not far from the creek where, as children, we swung on a rope-swing
that hung loose around the branch of an old gum
                         like a noose

she told me to shut up—those things didn't happen anymore
and that the old lady's name was ethel

iii.
my cousin didn't like my reply when she told me her house was haunted
—so she asked for a second opinion

she had her priest come over with holy water and exorcise her house,
                    had her psychic friend do another round

that night, resting peacefully in her no-longer 'haunted' house
my cousin dreamed of the australia that the history books taught her
she forgot the stories we were told under glistening stars with dark
shadows bouncing off the light of the campfire: stories of death,
of stolen babies, of blood-soaked land

she forgot:
that all land on this land, since the landing of the white man
                                has been haunted

Black Magic

BAKER BOY (FT. DALLAS WOODS)

Black Magic
Either you do or don't have it,
Young black and gifted, I'm talking the whole package
Magic magic lights camera action
You are now witnessing the power of
Black Magic

[Verse 1: Baker Boy]
Beŋur bili limurr bunhamirr
Nhuma marrtji monhamirr
Yol bili nhe yol bili ŋarra ga yol bili limurr mala
Gaŋga barrari nhuŋuwuy nhe
Nhäma nhe ga yäku yindi mala ŋunhi walal balanya bili
     nhakun ŋarra ga nhe
Yaka goraŋur dälthi gumurr'yurr
     ga badak gi marrtji marrtji marrtji
Yolthu nhuŋu dhu dhukarr gungam liw'maraŋ ga djudup
     dhawat gi
How long have we been fighting
Now you're all forgetting
Who you are and who I am and who we all are
As for you, don't fear
See the famous big name people they're just like you and me
No shame go hard front up be brave
     and just keep moving moving moving
Whoever blocks your road go around in and out

160

Then you will be known as unstoppable beast
We used to be together living happily beautiful weather
Thought it was forever
Calling home I'll be there soon
Yaka warguyurr ŋarra dhu märram nhumalany
napurr dhu ga latjukumnha nhina yalalany
Don't worry I'll come and get yous
And we'll be alright soon

Reminiscing chilling fishing laying down eyes close ticking
    mission twisting flipping spitting yolŋu matha ga
Representing ŋarraku mala (*my people*) this is how I wanna
    live my walŋa (*life*)
Marr ga dhu ga proud nhina yapa arly
So the sisters will be proud

Black Magic …

[Pre-chorus]
Either you do or don't have it,
Young black and gifted, I'm talking the whole package
Magic magic lights camera action
You are now witnessing the power of
Black Magic

[Chorus]
Black Magic
Black Magic

You are now witnessing the power!

[Verse 2: Dallas Woods]
When we gonna see another Mabo someone who really cares
    about tomorrow
Not about where to get his next bottle
We need more Cathy Freemans
Possibly more free men
These days blacks getting locked up for no reason
Archie Roach and while I'm preaching
Arms for the beggarman they took our children away
    apparently for the better man
Now they take our land big money for the settlement
Kevin Rudd said sorry and they thought it would settle it
But that didn't settle shit middle finger to politicians
The day that they listen will be the day that I see a difference
Are my people of Wyndham gonna see a coffin or a prison
    they think that it's living but it isn't
See a different vision
Young black and talented we all fit the description
What time to be alive, boy, I die for my district
Vivid picture the lyrical Namatjira and I'm pointing at my
    skin Nicky Winmar boy you know I'm

Black Magic

[Pre-chorus]
Either you do or don't have it,
Young black and gifted, I'm talking the whole package
Magic magic lights camera action
You are now witnessing the power of
Black Magic

[Chorus]
Black Magic

Black Magic

You are now witnessing the power!

[Verse 3: Baker Boy and Dallas Woods]
Dhuwana waluny nhuma dhu ganyim'thuna ŋarraku
    maɲinygu nhakun yolŋu balanda muḻkurrgu
This time you all gonna be in awe of me
    overpowered by the might like black and white minds
    combined

Black skin white skin centuries fighting straight to the point
Like I just dug the knife in

Throw me to the bush come out as a warrior
Put me in the city come out as the prime minister

If you don't wanna close the gap then close your gap,
A heated convo I'm cold like that

Magic ...

[Chorus]
Black Magic

Black Magic

You are now witnessing the power!

Better Put the Billy On

MAGGIE WALSH

Her voice —

Better put the billy on love
It's getting pretty late
And while you're out there getting more wood
Don't forget to shut that gate

His voice —

Well can you grab the Aerogard darl
It's sitting on the dash
These mozzies are biting pretty fierce
They're making me scratch 'n' scratch

And can you grab the harmonica too
It's on the back seat
I will play you a tune if you like
To forget this stifling heat

Her voice —

The stars are shining above
In the blue black sky
The glowing of a silver moon
Looking down from up high

The flickering of the campfire
It lights up the trees
With an eerily orange glow
The leaves rustle in the breeze

His voice —

The billy has started to boil! Time to add the tea leaves
Then let it sit on ground
Take that gumleaf out
Then swing billy round 'n' round

Both —

Into our enamel pannikins
Billy tea so hot and steaming
Across the rocks and plains
Moonlight shines down full beaming

And with that we'll have our fist sips
And follow it with a sigh
Then look up at the stars
That sparkle in the sky

Her voice —

Under the embers and dirt
The damper bakes away
My belly starts to grumble
Trying to keep hunger at bay

It must be nearly ready
It's been in there a while
As I begin to uncover our feed
I smell the aroma and smile

At my well-cooked damper
Brown 'n' char all round
I tap it lightly with a stick
And keep it warm on ground

His voice —

Yeah time to have a good old feed
Billy tea and damper tonight
Just let that butter melt into it
Then spread with vegemite

And now to wile away our evening
Here's another tune
On my trusty old harmonica
For you and the listening moon

Notes on Sources

'Hey Ancestor!' by Alexis Wright first appeared on IndigenousX, 24 January 2018.

'Beautiful Yuroke Red River Gum' by Lisa Bellear first appeared in *Dreaming in Urban Areas*, UQP, 1996.

'The Colour of Massacre' by Jeanine Leane first appeared in *States of Poetry ACT – Series One*, ed. Jen Webb, *Australian Book Review*, 2016.

'Unearth' by Ali Cobby Eckermann first appeared in *The Intervention: An Anthology*, eds Scott R and Heiss A, Concerned Australians, 2015.

'Domestic' by Natalie Harkin first appeared in *Dirty Words*, Cordite Books, 2015.

'Took the Children Away' by Archie Roach first appeared on the album *Charcoal Lane*, 1990. Written by A. Roach (Mushroom Music).

'The Children Came Back' by Briggs (ft. Gurrumul Yunupingu) first appeared on triple j's 'Like A Version' with the support of Reconciliation Australia, 2015. Words and music by Corey McGregor, James Mangohig, Archie Roach, Adam Briggs and Gurrumul Yunupingu: © 2014 Sony/ATV Music Publishing Allegro (Aust) Pty Ltd and SFM Publishing Pty Ltd (ABN 93 080 392 230) Locked Bag 7300, Darlinghurst NSW 1300.

'Yúya Karrabúrra (Fire Is Burning)' by Alice Eather first appeared
on ABC's 'The Word' and was first published in *Growing Up
Aboriginal in Australia*, ed. Heiss A, Black Inc., 2018.

'Bilya Kep' by Deborah Doorlak L. Moody was first performed
at 'Bilya Kep Waangkiny' ('River Water Stories') presented by
Community Arts Network Western Australia.

'Black Woman' by Ruby Langford Ginibi first appeared in
'Land and Identity: Proceedings of the 1997 Conference held
at The University of New England, Armidale, New South
Wales 27–30 September 1991', *Association for the Study
of Australian Literature*, eds Deves M and McDonell J A,
Armidale, 1998.

'A Letter to the Shade of Charles Darwin' by Jack Davis first
appeared in *Black Life: Poems*, UQP, 1992.

'The Grounding Sentence' by Samuel Wagan Watson first
appeared in *Love Poems and Death Threats*, UQP, 2014.

'Caused Us To Be Collaborator' and 'Connoisseur' by Lionel
Fogarty first appeared in *Eelahroo (Long Ago) Nyah (Looking)
Möbö-Möbö (Future)*, Vagabond Press, 2014.

'Darkinjung Burning' by Luke Patterson first appeared in *Plum Wood Mountain*, vol. 6, no. 2, 2019.

'Many Girls White Linen' by Alison Whittaker first appeared in *Overland 226*, 2017.

'Municipal Gum' by Oodgeroo Noonuccal first appeared in *The Dawn Is at Hand*, Jacaranda Press, 1966. Copyright © Estate of Oodgeroo Noonuccal. Reproduced with permission of John Wiley & Sons Ltd.

'Millad Mob Da Best!' by Diwurruwurru (with Phillip Hall) first appeared in *Rabbit*, no. 21, 2017. Diwurruwurru is a First Australians storytellers group, also called the Borroloola Poetry Club, and is located in the Northern Territory's Gulf of Carpenteria. Diwurruwurru is Yanyuwa for message stick and is used with permission from the Traditional Owners.

'YILAALU – BU-GADI (Once Upon a Time in the Bay of Gadi)' by Lorna Munro first appeared in *The Disappearing*, Red Room Poetry.

'Moorditj Yorgah' by Alf Taylor was first performed at 'Bilya Kep Waangkiny' ('River Water Stories') presented by Community Arts Network Western Australia.

'The New True Anthem' by Kevin Gilbert first appeared in *Inside Black Australia: An Anthology of Aboriginal Poetry*, Penguin, 1988.

'Boots' by Elizabeth Hodgson first appeared as 'I have an obsession with polished boots' in *Skin Painting*, UQP, 2008.

'Ngayrayagal Didjurigur (Soon Enough)' by Joel Davison first appeared in *Poetry in First Languages*, Red Room Poetry.

'Expert' by Ellen van Neerven first appeared in *Overland 223*, 2016.

'Dropbear Poetics' by Evelyn Araluen first appeared in *Overland 230*, 2018.

'Honey to Lips Bottlebrush' by Charmaine Papertalk Green first appeared in *False Claims of Colonial Thieves*, Magabala Books, 2018.

'Invasion Day' by Elizabeth Jarrett was first delivered as a speech on 26 January 2016 at a rally on Gadigal Country.

'Native Tongue' by Mojo Ruiz de Luzuriaga first appeared on the album *Native Tongue* by Mojo Juju, produced by Joelistics, ABC Music, 2018.

'Why Not Be Brothers and Sisters?' by Steven Oliver was first performed on 28 September 2014 at the Queensland Australian Poetry Slam finals at the State Library of Queensland.

'Got Ya' by Kerry Reed-Gilbert first appeared in *States of Poetry ACT – Series Two*, ed. Jen Webb, *Australian Book Review*, 2017.

'Nanna Emily's Poem (Mount Isa Cemetery 2014)' by Declan Furber Gillick first appeared as 'Mount Isa Cemetery 2015' on *Audacious Vol. 2: the audio-journal of Melbourne Spoken Word*, Melbourne Spoken Word.

'Are You Beautiful Today?' by Romaine Moreton first appeared in *How2*, vol. 1, no. 5, 2001.

'Say My Name' by Meleika Gesa-Fatafehi first appeared on *Djed Press*, djedpress.com and was first performed at the National Young Writers Festival in 2018.

'I Am the Road' by Claire G. Coleman first appeared in *Overland 226*, October 2018.

'Old Clever Woman' by Ken Canning/Burraga Gutya first appeared in *Yimbama*, Vagabond Press, 2015.

'The Changing Face of the Jukurrpa' by Pansy Rose Napaljarri first appeared in *Ngoonjook, Journal of Australian Indigenous Issues*, no. 10, August 1994, Batchelor Institute Press.

'Cult-charr Jammer' by Paul Collis first appeared in *States of Poetry ACT – Series Three*, ed. Jen Webb, *Australian Book Review*, 2018,

'Move on Black' by Jim Everett first appeared in *The Spirit of Kuti Kina: Tasmanian Aboriginal Poetry*, eds Everett J and Borwn K, Eumarrah Publications, 1990.

'My Ancestors' by Sachem Parkin-Owens first appeared in *Overland 226*, 2017.

'Justice for Youth' by Dylan Voller first appeared in *Honi Soit*, The University of Sydney, 2016, following his featuring on the *Four Corners* episode 'Australia's Shame', which exposed the mistreatment of Indigenous young offenders in Don Dale Detention Centre.

'Remember' by Laniyuk was shortlisted for the Nakata Brophy Short Fiction and Poetry Prize for Young Indigenous Writers, *Overland* 2017.

'Wirritjiribin' by Kirli Saunders first appeared in *Kindred*, Magabala Books, 2019.

'Haunted House' by Raelee Lancaster first appeared in *Overland 231*, 2018.

'Black Magic' by Baker Boy (ft. Dallas Woods) was first released as a single in July 2018.

'Better Put the Billy On' by Maggie Walsh first appeared in *Sunset*, Vagabond Press, 2016.

Acknowledgements

The University of Queensland Press (UQP) acknowledges the Turrbul and Jagera peoples as the traditional custodians of the land on which UQP operates. We pay our respects to their Ancestors and their descendants, who continue cultural and spiritual connections to Country. We recognise their valuable contributions to Australian and global society.

UQP would like to thank: the Copyright Agency's Cultural Fund for their support of this project; Meleika Gesa-Fatafehi for being a wonderful editorial assistant, especially in the early stages of this book; Rachael Sarra for the fabulous cover illustration; and The Garret podcast (and host extraordinaire, Astrid Edwards) for allowing us to reproduce much of their interview with Ali Cobby Eckermann. And publisher Aviva Tuffield would particularly like to pay tribute to Alison Whittaker for generously taking on the curatorship of this book, and for her intelligence, insight and sensitivity every step of the way.

Alison would like to acknowledge the Nations and Elders on whose Country the works herein were written; the Nations of the poets themselves; and the long line of First Nations poets before each of us that made our work possible. Alison edited this collection on Gadigal, Wangal and Gomeroi Country.

This project was called *Fire Front* to describe the various power, restoration and dynamism of Indigenous verse. During 2019 and 2020, as it came together, this continent was beset by catastrophic and unprecedented fires escalated by climate change, colonisation, and depriving First Nations of their right to care for Country. We chose to keep the name, so we wouldn't forget two things: what the words of Aboriginal and Torres Strait Islander poems are and can do, and what their poets stand to lose.